ATHENS

- A ☑ in the text denotes a highly recommended sight
- A complete A–Z of practical information starts on p.115
- Extensive mapping throughout: on cover flaps and in text

Copyright © **1995** by Berlitz Publishing Co Ltd, Berlitz House, Peterley Road, Oxford OX4 2TX, England, and Berlitz Publishing Company Inc., 257 Park Avenue South, New York, NY 10010, USA.

All rights reserved. No part of this book may be reproduced or transmitted in any form or by any means, electronic or mechanical, including photocopying, recording or by any information storage and retrieval system without permission in writing from the publisher.

Berlitz Trademark Reg. US Patent Office and other countries. Marca Registrada.

Printed in Switzerland by Weber SA, Bienne.

18th edition (1995/1996)

Although we make every effort to ensure the accuracy of the information in this guide, changes do occur. If you have any new information, suggestions or corrections to contribute, we would like to hear from you. Please write to Berlitz Publishing at one of the above addresses.

Text:	Donna Dailey
Editors:	Delphine Verroest, Donald Greig
Photography:	Donna Dailey, except p.103 by Luc Chessex
Layout:	Suzanna Boyle
Cartography:	*Falk* Falk Verlag, Hamburg and Visual Image
Thanks to:	Thomson Airfares, Thomson City Breaks, Chat Tours and G.O. Tours for their invaluable assistance in the preparation of this guide.

Cover photographs: Front: *The Acropolis* © Tony Stone Images
Back: *Temple of Jupiter* © Tony Stone Images

CONTENTS

Athens and the Athenians

Athens is Europe's southernmost capital city, and the gateway to Greece and the ancient world. Its renowned hallmark is the gleaming marble of the monuments of the Acropolis, which rise triumphantly above the city, proud survivors of the ravages of man and time. People have dwelt on this rock for some 5,000 years – a lineage so ancient as to make all other European cities seem young by comparison. Below, in the ancient Agora, or marketplace, Socrates held his dialogues, and the system of democracy we know today had its beginning, making Athens the cradle of Western civilization. It is this rich history that continues to act as a magnet for travellers throughout the world.

Modern Athens is far removed from the elegant splendour of its classical ruins. The low sprawl of steel and concrete stretches up into the surrounding hills as far as the eye can see. (Remarkably for a city of this size, there are no skyscrapers and under a dozen tall buildings.) Aesthetics have fallen by the wayside during the 20th century, for a massive influx of rural Greeks and repatriated countrymen from Turkey has made a necessity of rapid (and frenzied) growth. Today, metropolitan Athens, along with the adjoining city and port of Piraeus, is home to 4 million people, a figure that equals nearly half the population of the entire country.

You will most likely arrive during the chaos of daytime Athens, with your first glimpse of the Acropolis through a haze of heat and smog. Frightful traffic, clogged streets, air and noise pollution, and sweltering summer temperatures can be as trying here as in any large city at this latitude. Head straight for Plaka, the oldest quarter of town, plant yourself at a shady café table and relax. You will soon adjust to the city's cacophonous rhythms.

Plaka is a real kaleidoscope of unexpected delights. At any turning along its warren-like **5**

streets, you may come across a drama troupe rehearsing ancient Greek tragedy in a back garden, or a trio of old men strumming guitars and singing folk songs around a rickety pavement table.

Athens is about such moments: a breezy respite on a roof garden, a lunchtime accordion serenade, a fresh rose from a flower seller on a rare, rainy day, and the play of the late afternoon light on the Parthenon. At this time of day, looking down from the Acropolis, even the roaring concrete

forest below can seem magnificent. Such moments will be savoured long after any tour of the ancient marbles has ended.

Athens is at its best at night; when the cool evening breezes alleviate the heat and noise of the day, the atmosphere gives way to that of an enticing cosmopolitan city tempered by island *bonhomie*. The Athenians shrug off the stress and struggles of urban life and meet up with friends at a local *platía* (square) or *kafeníon* (coffee shop). Now is the time to stroll through the brightly lit Plaka amid chattering crowds... to let the wafting odours of broiling meat whet your appetite, and to stop for a meal on a pretty patio strung with grapevines and flowers, where you dine to the strains of *bouzoúki* music.

Crossroads

Like a mournful Greek ballad, Athenian culture has various strands influenced by East and West, embracing progress but revering tradition. The Byzantine chanting which drifts out of churches, the black-robed and bearded Orthodox priests, and the strange, almost pictographic letters of the Greek alphabet give the city a slightly exotic air. Saints' days are celebrated with wreaths of white flowers, as Athenians in business suits line up solemnly to kiss the icon, and holidays are marked with lively folk dancing and processions. That the Athenians uphold their heritage in the midst of a modern metropolis is befitting of a people whose forefathers advanced the concept of a 'city' from the very beginning.

It is fitting, too, that the venerable monuments of Athens, built by those ancient citizens, should still stand in the viable heart of their progeny. Historian TW Rolleston wrote: 'The elements which in the most remote times have entered into a nation's composition endure through all its history, and help to mould that history, and to stamp the character and genius of the people.'

The Greeks are a volatile, talkative, irrepressibly curious people. They pamper their babies and honour their grand-parents. Their pride is quiet and dignified. You'll see men walking arm in arm and arguing passionately – a favourite pastime – and every now and then, amid the conglomerate of Athenian faces – small and round, dark or fair – you will notice those same, finely chis-

*P*laka's pretty houses and lively cafés constitute an atmospheric diversion below the Acropolis.

A lace seller shows off her wares (above). The marble splendours of the Roman Forum (right).

elled features that, for centuries, have gazed proudly from classical statues.

Greek hospitality is both warm and genuine. It is a tradition, too, which goes back to ancient times, when the belief was that passing strangers may have been gods in disguise. At the same time you'll come to respect the local business acumen, whether you're buying a flea-market trinket or trying to charter a yacht. Athenians, in the tradition of cunning classical Greek hero Odysseus, have sharp minds. They place a high value on education, and many speak several languages. In addition, most have acquired at least a rudimentary knowledge of English.

Greeks come to their capital from the islands and all around the mainland for a variety of reasons, but primarily to study, work, and make a better life for themselves and their families. As a result, over the years the city has become a microcosm of Greek culture, not to mention the beneficiary of the country's natural and human resources. Take, for instance, the spectacular quantity and use of marble. An astounding thirty percent of the surface area of this mountainous country is pure marble – 130 different kinds, of all colours and quality. It is this variety which gives the monuments and statues of Athens such splendour.

Athens Today

Although Greece has for long been one of the poorer countries of Europe, its fortunes are changing. The Greek economy is based on the dollar, and even though the devaluation of the drachma has brought inflation, most Athenians are now enjoying a higher standard of living than ever before. European Union (previously European Community) membership has brought with it modernization in banking and civil services, and funds for improving the transport system, including the new subway lines which are being built across the city.

The strong bonds of family, religion and nationalism have largely insulated Greece from the sort of social problems that plague other European countries. Drugs, alcoholism and homelessness were practically unheard of until recent years and even now are seldom seen. This is one aspect of modern life in which Athens is content to lag behind. Urban crime

*T*he modern and the traditional – fishing boats and luxury yachts dock at Zéa Harbour in Piraeus.

of Piraeus, third largest in the Mediterranean. Stand on deck on the huge island ferries that sail in and out of here, and you will marvel at its scope. Along with tourism and agriculture, the merchant navy is one of Greece's three main industries.

Athens has always been a world crossroads. Having dealt with invaders throughout its history, the city has coped well with the tourist bombardment of recent years (Greece expected 10 million visitors in 1994). Even those heading for the islands often spend at least a night or two in Athens, and for many, this is a destination in its own right. If the urban din gets too much, mountain villages, get-away islands and beaches are easily accessible.

Athens, a city very much on the move, absorbs effortlessly its waves of visitors, while straining its Hellenic ingenuity for greater commercial and industrial prominence. Yet in the end, regardless of how modern it becomes or the extent of the progress it achieves, it will always uphold the splendid heritage evoked by its very name.

rates are still low, making it one of the safest capitals in Europe you can visit.

The city centre lies just over 6km (4 miles) from the sea, where the wealth and glory of ancient Athens was forged out of fierce naval battles and rich trade. This great seafaring tradition still thrives at the port

A Brief History

Athens' legendary history begins with a contest between Athena, goddess of wisdom, and Poseidon, god of the sea. Both had their eye on the city, so it was agreed that whoever could come up with the more useful gift for mortals would win. The half-human, half-serpent king of Athens, Cecrops, acted as arbiter.

The contest started with Poseidon, who struck the rock of the Acropolis with his mighty trident and brought salt water gushing forth. Athena offered an olive tree, however, which proved more valuable, and so she acquired the position of the city's special protector.

The history of the city is just as fascinating. From around 2000 BC, wandering bands filtered into Athens and other parts of Greece from western

Russia or Asia Minor. Known as Achaeans, they were the first Greek-speaking people in the area, and over the centuries they built many imposing fortresses and developed the rich Mycenaean civilization based in the Peloponnesus. In the minor Acropolis of Athens a wall and palace were built.

The Achaeans' chief rivals and mentors were the dazzling Minoans of Crete – that is until about 1450 BC when their empire was devastated, possibly by tidal waves caused by the eruption of the volcanic island of Thera (Santorini). For several centuries, the Mycenaeans dominated the eastern Mediterranean and Aegean. A long

*S*cenes on traditional black-figure pottery illustrate legendary warriors and heroes.

series of conflicts, however, including the legendary siege of Troy, weakened these mighty mainland warriors.

Around 1100 BC waves of Dorians swept into the area on horseback. Armed with iron spears and shields, they overpowered the Bronze Age chariots of Mycenae and broke down the Peloponnesian bastions. The ensuing 'dark ages' lasted about three centuries.

Somehow, Athens managed to escape the scourge, but only after 700 BC did it take over and lift to unimagined heights the heritage of Mycenae and Crete. Although they warred as often as they united with each other, Athenians, Spartans, Thebans and many others shared a real sense of identity. They were all Greeks – they shared a common tongue and an evolving pan-Hellenic religion, and at regular intervals they were brought together by the ritual athletic contest of the Olympian, Delphian and Isthmian games.

Athens was the largest city-state and gradually embraced all of the Attica peninsula.

King Theseus, the legendary ruler who slayed the minotaur in the Cretan labyrinth (see p.91), was revered by Athenians for bringing Attica's scattered and independent villages under the rule of the Acropolis. Countless urns and jars were decorated with drawings of his heroic exploits, but in fact he belongs to myth rather than history. The villages actually merged with Athens in exchange for protection, a share of state offices and full citizenship rights.

From Aristocracy to Democracy

During the dark ages Athens had been a monarchy, but it emerged as an oligarchy in the 7th century BC. The first great historical figure of that new era was Solon – general, merchant, poet and sage – who in 594 BC became chief magistrate. At that time, civil war threatened to break out between the city-state's 'haves' and 'have nots' (an expression from ancient Greece). Armed with almost absolute powers,

HISTORICAL LANDMARKS

1100-800 BC	The Dark Age.
776-480 BC	The Archaic Period.
621-593 BC	Draco and Solon codify Athenian laws.
508 BC	Cleisthenes introduces democracy in Athens.
490 BC	First Persian War. Greeks succeed at Marathon.
480-338 BC	The Classical Period.
480 BC	Athens plundered, but Persians defeated in the Strait of Salamis.
477 BC	Athens unites allies under the League of Delos.
459-429 BC	The Golden Age of Pericles.
447-438 BC	The Parthenon is built on the Acropolis.
431-404 BC	Peloponnesian War. Athens defeated by Sparta.
338-146 BC	The Hellenistic Period.
338 BC	Philip II of Macedon defeats Athens at Chaeronea.
336-323 BC	Alexander the Great rules Greece.
149-146 BC	Greece falls under Roman rule.
AD 50	St Paul brings Christianity to Athens.
AD 128	Emperor Hadrian rebuilds Athens.
AD 324	Constantinople becomes capital of Eastern Empire.
1456	Athens falls to the Turks, beginning four centuries of Ottoman rule.
1821-32	Greek War of Independence.
1833	Athens becomes the capital of Greece.
1922	Repatriated Greeks flood into Athens.
1941-44	Nazi Germany occupies Greece.
1944-49	Greek Civil War ends with Communist defeat.
1951	Greece becomes a member of NATO.
1967-74	Military junta rules Greece.
1981	Greece joins the Common Market.

Solon produced a constitution advancing the ideal of equality before the law for citizens of all classes, set up a trial-by-jury system, freed the peasantry from debt to landowners, and introduced far-sighted reforms which revived the languishing economy.

In the middle of the 6th century, Athens' first dictator took power. Peisistratus established a dynasty which held on to power – with interruptions –

for half a century. (Forced out on one occasion, he dressed a tall, beautiful country girl to look like Athena, before entering Athens in triumph with the 'goddess' leading a procession.) He was a resourceful tyrant, who steered Athens towards greatness, and under his rule, commerce and the arts flourished: Attica's wine and olive oil were shipped to Italy, Egypt and Asia Minor in beautiful black-figure pots; the first tragedies ever written were performed at the annual festival of the wine god, Dionysus, and the standard version of Homer's works was set down.

Peisistratus' sons, who succeeded him, proved less popular, and so after some time democracy was eventually re-established. Cleisthenes, who was the true founder of Athenian democracy, took over in 508 BC. An aristocrat by birth, he introduced electoral con-

The remains of the Concert Hall of Agrippa stand amid trees and flowers in the ancient Agora.

sistuencies called *demes* and set up a sovereign citizens' assembly and a senate, whose members were chosen by lot. He also introduced an inspired system of 'ostracism', under which any citizen who became dangerously too big for his boots could be banished from Athens for ten years, but without loss of property.

The Persian Wars

At the end of the 5th century BC, Greece entered the period of the Persian Wars, as recorded in Herodotus' great narrative *History* of the ancient world (see p.43).

The Persian Empire's far-flung lands included a number of Greek settlements on the coast of what is now Turkey. When the Greek towns attempted a revolt in 499 BC, Athens sent an expedition to aid their uprising. The revolt failed, but Persian King Darius could not let such impudence go unpunished, and in 490 BC he confidently launched an invasion of Attica. Although the Persians' forces and resources were vastly superior, Darius hadn't anticipated the amazing courage and battlefield skill of the Greeks.

A fleet of around 600 Persian vessels landed at Marathon Beach. Led by General Miltiades, the Athenians inflicted a crippling and humiliating defeat on the Persians. According to legend, the soldier who ran from Marathon to Athens – a distance of 42km – died of exhaustion after reporting the victory. His feat is still commemorated today in the 42km (26-mile) Olympic race known as the marathon.

When Darius' son, Xerxes, re-invaded Greece by land and sea in far greater strength ten years later, the Greeks' defeat seemed inevitable. However, a few hundred heroic troops under Leonidas of Sparta delayed the enormous Persian army at the pass of Thermopylae long enough for Athens to be evacuated to the island of Salamis. Vowing to avenge his father's defeat, Xerxes seized and plundered the city, burning down all the wooden structures on the Acropolis. **15**

Divine Dozen

Every Greek schoolchild can reel off the names and particulars of the family of 12 top deities on Mount Olympus:

Zeus. Supreme ruler of the gods and men, protector of Greece, master of the weather; his symbols are the eagle and the oak tree. **Hera**. Zeus's third and oft-betrayed wife, protectress of marriage, mothers and the home. **Athena**. Daughter of Zeus, goddess of wisdom, guardian of war heroes, who reputedly invented the flute and the potter's wheel. **Apollo**. Son of Zeus, god of the sun, music, healing and prophecy (his advice was sought at the oracle of Delphi). **Artemis**. Twin sister of Apollo, goddess of hunting and the moon, guardian of women and cities. **Hermes**. Son of Zeus, messenger of the gods, the god of commerce, orators and writers; protector of flocks, thieves and travellers. **Ares**. Son of Zeus, god of war, unpopular on Olympus and feared by the Greeks.

Hephaestus. Son of Zeus, god of fire and industry, the lame blacksmith of the gods who supplied Zeus with thunderbolts. **Aphrodite**. Daughter of Zeus, goddess of love, beauty and gardens, the most beautiful goddess of Olympus. **Poseidon**. Zeus's brother, god of seas, rivers, and earthquakes, who caused storms with his trident and moved to an undersea Aegean palace when defeated by Zeus for control of the sky; giver of horses to man. **Demeter**. Sister of Zeus, goddess of agriculture, protectress of crops, gave men corn and the plough. **Hestia**. Zeus's elder sister, beloved goddess of fire and the hearth, protectress of the home, family and city.

Other notable gods are **Dionysus**, Zeus' son by a mortal, god of wine, revelry and hospitality; **Asklepios**, Apollo's son, god of healing; and **Hades**, ruler of the kingdom of the dead.

He then climbed a hill, from where he could watch his fleet of 700 ships engage Themistocles' much smaller naval force in the Strait of Salamis. With the aid of brilliant tactics and newer ships, though, the Greek fleet managed to trounce the Persians. That crucial battle of 480 BC turned the tide.

The final, decisive battle of the Persian Wars took place at Platae, where Xerxes' troops were soundly beaten. Greek independence had been preserved again, and with it the foundations on which Western civilization has been built.

The Golden Age

For almost 50 years, peace reigned at home and the victorious city-state knew its most magnificent era. Transforming a maritime league into an empire, Athens amassed 'protection money' from its 'subject allies'. The resources of the treasury were used – among other things – to build in perpetual marble the Parthenon and other monuments that still adorn the Acropolis today.

The moving power behind this unrivalled time of greatness – the Golden Age – was Pericles. This liberal-inclined aristocrat was, in effect, the supreme ruler of Athens and its empire for 30 years, until his death in 429 BC.

Innumerable works of art, literature, science and philosophy of great and lasting worth were produced by what Pericles referred to as the 'school of Hellas'. The geniuses we

With Eros close at hand, Aphrodite fends off Pan with her sandal (c. 100 BC).

see memorialized in marble busts and street names in Athens today were often close personal friends of the great ruler: the dramatists Euripides and Sophocles, and the historian Herodotus, for example, along with philosopher Socrates and the brilliant scientists Zeno and Anaxagoras. The first literary salon in history was held by Aspasia, Pericles' mistress, who was a remarkable woman of intelligence and spirit.

During all this, the Athenian political system allowed the average *citizen* a greater degree of participation in public life than ever before anywhere, and perhaps since. Of course, the number of citizens (free adult males) was small – probably not above 30,000 – while the population as a whole, including women, children, resident aliens and slaves, might have been ten times as great.

Slavery was common, and justified on the grounds that 'democracy' could not exist unless the citizens were free to devote themselves to the service of the state. Most slaves in Athens were war prisoners.

The Peloponnesian War

As Athens prospered, intense economic and ideological rivalry developed with Greece's other powerful city-state and ally during the Persian Wars, Sparta. In 431 BC the Peloponnesian War broke out between them. For 27 years the debilitating conflict dragged on, involving most of the Greek world. Yet literature and art continued to flourish in spite of the incessant fighting, and during this time Athens built two of the loveliest temples on the Acropolis, the Erechtheion and the temple to Athena Nike (see pp.34 and 29).

Finally Sparta, with naval help from former foe Persia, blockaded what was then the Hellespont (now the Dardanelles Strait), thus cutting off Athens from its crucial supply of corn. Starvation and heavy naval losses proved too much for Athens, and the Spartans claimed total victory.

Sparta attempted to govern the city through a council of 30 men, who were known as the Thirty Tyrants and who spent most of their time persecuting opponents and confiscating property. In less than a year they were driven from the city, and Sparta, embroiled in other conflicts, let Athens reestablish its maritime alliances without resistance.

Nonetheless, Athens' days as a great political power were over. As internal feuding led to a weakening of power, a new star rose in the north – that of Philip II of Macedon, father of Alexander the Great. He advanced the far-sighted scheme of a federation of Greek states, which Athens resisted for a long period. Some Athenians even urged the Assembly to declare war on the Macedonian King. (The fiery *Philippics* – speeches on the subject – by master orator Demosthenes, rate among the finest of their kind.) After losing the battle of Chaeronea in 338 BC, however, the Athenians accepted an alliance with other states and even sent Philip a gold crown as a token of submission.

Culturally and intellectually, though, Athens remained unsurpassed through the 4th century and thus the capital of Greek civilization. Aristotle, the towering thinker with one of history's most encyclopaedic minds, held forth at his own school of the Lyceum; Menander wrote comic plays; Praxiteles sculpted scores of superb statues (including that of *Hermes*, which he called 'of no account' but which is probably the greatest Greek sculpture in existence – on view in the museum at Olympia). This age, in fact, had an even more lasting influence on Rome and Byzantium, and through them on medieval and Renaissance Europe, than that exerted by Athens during its great 'classical' 5th century (see p.43).

Roman Rule

As the centre of power shifted from Athens to Alexandria, Macedonian troops occupied Athens twice – first in 322 and then in 262 BC. However, the Macedonian Empire could not survive long after Alexander's death. Eventually, after a series of wars, it was dismantled **19** by the far-ranging legions of Rome. Macedonia became just another Roman province (in 146 BC) and Athens not much more than a showplace museum city – though its philosophy schools and orators kept attracting Romans with political ambitions. Cicero and Horace spent student years in Athens, and Emperor Hadrian is said to have been initiated into the sacred mysteries of Demeter at Eleusis (the most famous secret religious rites of ancient Greece, see p.84).

Although generally treated well throughout some five centuries of Pax Romana, Athens suffered severely on one occasion. In 86 BC, Roman general Sulla sacked the city in retribution for its unwise alliance with Mithridates, King of Pontus and bitter enemy of Rome. Many Athenian treasures were carried off to Italy.

Athens' good fortune was that the Romans held Greek culture in such high esteem. Most notable was the Emperor Hadrian (AD 76-138), who had a love of classical Greek architecture. Among other monuments, he erected his distinctive arched gate and completed the temple of Olympian Zeus, on foundations laid by Peisistratus nearly seven centuries earlier (see p.41).

Byzantine and Ottoman Obscurity

Roman Emperor Constantine gave Christianity official sanction, and in 326 he chose as his 'New Rome' the former Greek colonial town of Byzantium, since dubbed Constantinople. Athens thus lost all chance of becoming the chief city of the eastern Mediterranean. Under Byzantine rule the city of Pericles sank into deep provincial obscurity. Devastated once by rampaging Goths (in AD 267), it otherwise merited only a few brief mentions in the history of the following centuries.

Christianity had taken early root in Greece, as a result of a visit to Athens made by St Paul somewhere around AD 50. Polytheism, however, persisted until 529, when an edict by Emperor Justinian shut down the last 'pagan' temples and the famous Athenian schools of philosophy.

During the 13th and 14th centuries, Athens found itself governed by a number of adventurers from Florence, Catalonia and Burgundy.

Athens and Attica was taken by the Turks in 1456, three years after these new empire-builders had seized Constantinople. In the following four centuries of oppressive Ottoman rule – now known as Greece's darkest age – Athens was all but forgotten. Through this difficult period, only the Orthodox Church could provide its people with any sense of continuity.

The city was twice briefly taken away from the Turks by the Venetians: first in 1466, and then again in 1687, when one of their shells hit a munitions store in the Parthenon. This did, in fact, badly damage the 2,000-year-old structure.

Traditional évzones mark the changing of the guard outside Greece's Parliament building.

Independence

Athens dwindled ever further. When the English poet Lord Byron visited it in 1809, he found that what had once been the glittering centre of the civilized world now had a population of only about 5,000 souls.

Starting on 25 March 1821, when Archbishop Germanos of Patras raised a new blue and white banner and declared independence, it took 11 years and some formidable foreign help for the Greeks to win their war against Turkish rule. Both Athens and the Acropolis changed hands more than once during the long struggle in which many English, Scots, Irish and French fought alongside the Greeks. Byron, who popularized the cause abroad, died at Missolonghi in 1824 (of disease, and not fighting).

On 27 October 1827, the Greek revolution was won, but the last Turks weren't evicted from the Acropolis until 1833. The following year, the little town of Athens was declared the capital of modern Greece. Theoretically sovereign, the new state was an artificial creation: the 17-year-old Bavarian Prince Otto had been installed as king by the Great Powers. He and his queen, Amalia, were deposed in 1862, but during his reign Athens slowly returned to being a city again and Greece made considerable economic progress.

As a result of complex European diplomatic talks, a second adolescent came to the Greek throne in 1863, the 18-year-old William of the Danish royal house, Schleswig-Holstein-Sonderburg-Glückburg). He took the name George I, King of the Hellenes, and remained in power for 50 years until his assassination in 1913.

The 20th Century

The events which have made up Greek history throughout the past century have been as chaotic as any since the classical age. The dominant figure between 1910 and 1935 was Eleftherios Venizelos, a Cretan politician who was prime minister several times. He helped Greece regain Macedonia and most of the Aegean islands, including Crete itself and Epirus in the northwest. He was also responsible for the population exchange agreement with Turkey (1922), under which almost one million repatriated Greeks flooded into a woefully unprepared Athens. The desperate, makeshift effort to accommodate them pushed back the city's boundaries farther than ever before (accounting now for the oldest of the suburban eyesores in the capital).

From 1936 to 1940, Greece was under the military dictatorship of Ioannis Metaxas, remembered for the resounding *óchi* (no) he gave in reply to Mussolini's ultimatum to surrender in 1940. The Greeks commemorate the day, 28 October, as a national holiday.

Greece was invaded by Nazi Germany in April 1941 and by June the Germans controlled the entire country, with Italian forces placed in Athens. The people suffered greatly, but the city's monuments escaped serious damage. Unfortunately, the Greek resistance movement which was formed dur-

The Greek flag flies proudly over the capital from the heights of the Acropolis.

ing the war was so politically divided that the guerrillas expended almost as much energy fighting against each other as the Germans – a tragic situation familiar to students of the ancient city-states.

In October 1944, the Allied forces moved into Athens and much of Greece, encountering **23** little opposition from the retreating Germans.

The war left Greece utterly devastated, but factions still squabbled ceaselessly in an attempt to gain political advantage. Communist and royalist partisans moved inexorably toward military showdown as the United States, under the Truman Doctrine, sent the first instalment of economic aid. Two years of savage civil war ended in late 1949 with Communist defeat, but political instability was not resolved in Athens until a military dictatorship seized power in 1967.

During the seven-year reign of the colonels, political parties were dissolved, the press was censored and left-wing sympathizers were exiled, tortured and imprisoned. In November 1973, a student protest at the Athens Polytechnic was brutally crushed. This action spelled the end of Greek tolerance of the regime, which collapsed eight months later when the junta attempted to overthrow the Cypriot president, Archbishop Makarios, and instead provoked the Turkish invasion of Cyprus. Constantine Karamanlis, the former conservative premier, was recalled from exile in Paris to restore democracy. The reforms which followed brought the abolition of the monarchy, with a new constitution for a republican government then being drawn up in 1975.

With its entry into the Common Market in 1981, Greece's economic prospects strengthened. That same year, the first socialist government swept to victory under the leadership of Andréas Papandréou and the PASOK party. Papandréou espoused the desires of a postwar generation to maintain peace and stability, and secure a better future for their children. By 1990, beleaguered by personal and financial scandals in the administration, PASOK was defeated at the polls, after three rounds of voting, by the conservative New Democracy party, and Constantine Mitsotákis became the new prime minister. The victory turned out to be short-lived, however, for the tenacious Papandréou was re-elected in 1994.

What to See

The remains of ancient Greece are scattered throughout Athens. Often, you'll round a corner and come upon fragments of a column or the ruins of an ancient building. It is these unexpected discoveries that can make exploring the city such a delight. Take time to enjoy them; the summer heat will counter any tendency to rush.

The famous Greek temples and sculptures are at the top of every visitor's list, along with the later Roman monuments. Also beautiful and intriguing are the churches – both Orthodox and the few remaining jewels of the Byzantine era.

The main sights and museums are all within a short walk or bus ride of one another. Everywhere you'll get caught up in the vibrant and non-stop spectacle that is Athens today.

Some of Athens' hotel roof gardens offer splendid views of the city and the Acropolis.

The Acropolis

This 4ha (10-acre) rock rising 90m (300ft) above the plain of Attica reigns over Athens with timeless majesty. Its name is derived from Greek and means 'high town': *acro* – highest point and *polis* – town or city. It also means 'citadel'.

Stone Age man first inhabited the Acropolis more than 5,000 years ago. Strategically sited near a good, safe anchorage, it was accessible, defendable, commanded surrounding territory and had its own natural springs (more than 20 are known today). The rock was crowned by a thriving Mycenaean citadel in the Bronze Age, but in the 7th century BC the political and social life of the polis shifted to the *agorá* (marketplace) and the ancient fortress was transformed into a sacred place for worship of the gods. The first wooden temples were destroyed by the Persians in 480 BC (see p.15), but during the Golden Age of Pericles, the Acropolis was rebuilt with the splendid and enduring marble structures that can still be seen today.

The Acropolis is most beautiful (and best photographed) in the late afternoon light, when the descending sun gives the white monuments a shimmering golden hue. Many people prefer to visit during the cool hours of early morning (on summer days, few places in southern Europe seem as

*S*top to catch your breath ... a labyrinthine path leads through Anafiótika up to the Acropolis.

ATHENS HIGHLIGHTS

(See also Museum Highlights on p.57)

The Acropolis. Tel. 321-0219. Open Mon-Fri 8am-6.30pm, Sat-Sun 8.30am-2.45pm. Admission 1,500drs. This ancient citadel and landmark of Athens contains some of the world's finest monuments of antiquity, including the Parthenon and the Erechtheion, with its unusual Porch of the Caryatids. Admission includes entrance to the Acropolis Museum. There are wonderful views over Athens and the ancient Agora. (See p.26)

The Ancient Agora and the Temple of Hephaistos. Tel. 321-0185. Open Tues-Sun 8.30am-2.45pm. Closed Mon. Admission 800drs. Wander around the sprawling ruins of the ancient marketplace, where democracy and philosophy had their beginnings. The temple of Hephaistos – known as the Thisío – is one of the best preserved in Athens. Admission includes entrance to the Stoa of Attalus Museum. (See p.42)

The Temple of the Olympian Zeus. Vas. Olgas and Amalias Avenue; tel. 922-6330. Open Tues-Sun 8.30am-3pm. Closed Mon. Admission 400drs. Fifteen impressive Corinthian columns mark the remains of the largest temple ever built in ancient Greece. (See p.41)

Plaka. Athens' oldest quarter lies between Ermou Street and the Acropolis, and has lively shops and tavernas and colourful back streets perfect for wandering. Visit the Museum of Greek Folk Art and the lovely Tower of the Winds. (See p.45)

Churches. Of Athens' many churches, three 'must-sees' are Agíos Elefthérios, next to the cathedral; Kapnikaréa, on Ermou Street,and Agii Theódori at Klafthmónos Square. (See p.50)

Mount Lycabettus. For spectacular views of the city, take the cable car at the end of Ploutarchou in Kolonaki. (See p.55)

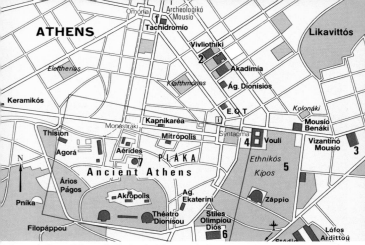

1 *Post Office*   2 *National Library*   3 *Byzantine Museum*   4 *Parliament*
5 *National Gardens*   6 *Temple of Olympian Zeus*   7 *Tower of the Winds*

blazingly hot as the Acropolis). Due to on-going restoration work, it is not possible to visit the summit at night. The Acropolis is open every day, though precise hours are subject to change (do check with the tourist office, see p.134). It is advisable to wear sensible shoes, as the steep marble entranceway can be slippery.

The path up to the entrance generally follows the ramped course of ancient processionals. These climaxed in the Greater Panathenaia, a festival held every four years on the night of the midsummer full moon to honour Athena, protectress of the city. Imagine, as you ascend, the great procession, which began north of the Agora and wound through the marketplace and up the Sacred Way. Taking part were garlanded priests and priestesses, musicians, cavalry troops and young maidens escorting a great ship on wheels carrying the *peplos*, a sacred embroidered saffron robe to adorn the statue of the goddess. Farm lads coaxed she-goats, ewes and heifers up the slope – for sacrifice to the virgin goddess. This glorious spectacle was rendered on the great frieze which once ran on all four sides of the Parthenon's inner temple.

The visitors' entrance is the Beulé Gate, a 3rd-century AD Roman addition. The imposing pedestal on the left of the path once supported a bronze four-horse Roman chariot (the *Agrippa*). From behind this high plinth, there is a superb view of the Agora and the Thisío temple (see p.44).

THE PROPYLAEA (*Propílea*)

Six Doric columns mark the monumental entrance to the Acropolis. More than a grand gateway, the function of the Propylaea was to generate awe and respect, and prepare lesser mortals for a meeting with the goddess. Construction began in 437 BC, but was halted five years later by the Peloponnesian War and never finished.

The central and largest of the gateways was intended for chariots and approached by a ramp; steps lead up to the four other entries. As you reach the porch, you'll see Ionic as well as Doric columns; this was the first building to incorporate both styles (compare the solid majesty of the Doric with the light elegance of the Ionic). The **Pinakotheke** on the left side housed a gallery of paintings done on wooden panels, depicting heroic deeds.

THE TEMPLE OF ATHENA NIKE (*Athiná Níki*)

This enchanting temple, with a graceful Ionic portico, perches high on a terrace off to the right (southwest) of the Propylaea, and has a glorious panorama of the sea and distant mountains. Built between 427 and 424 BC by the architect Callicrates, during a respite from the Peloponnesian War, it points towards the Parthenon, and was devoted to Athena as the goddess of peace and victory, the temple once housed a winged statue of her. One day, fearing their protectress would desert the city, the Athenians clipped the statue's wings; thus the temple is also called Wingless Victory. The temple **29** was torn down by the Turks in 1687 to make way for an artillery position; the one now standing was later painstakingly reassembled from the rubble by archaeologists during the 19th and 20th centuries.

Passing through the Propylaea, you come out onto the great sloping plateau of the Acropolis. Try to imagine the scene 2,400 years ago, when these masterworks of architecture and sculpture were going up. Scores of stone cutters, carpenters, founders and braziers, goldsmiths, ivory workers, painters, dyers, and even embroiderers swarmed over this ground. For the most part they were freemen, not slaves, practitioners of nearly every art and craft then known.

Dominating the immediate foreground was an enormous bronze statue of Athena under another guise – Athena Promachos, the Defender. This statue of the goddess holding shield and spear was created by Phidias to honour the victory at Marathon (see p.15). It's said that sailors could spot the tip of her helmet as their ships

sailed round the gulf from Soúnion. The statue stood here for 1,000 years, until it was carted off to Constantinople in the 6th century AD.

THE PARTHENON (*Parthenón*)

The French poet Lamartine called the Parthenon the 'most perfect poem in stone', and not even the scaffolding which is now in the inner sanctum (restoration work will continue into the next century) can mar the magnificent beauty of the greatest architectural achievement of classical Greece.

The Parthenon – meaning Temple of the Virgin – was dedicated to Athena, goddess of wisdom and justice, protectress of the city. It was designed by the sculptor Phidias using ancient principles of sacred numerology, geometry and architecture, and was executed by master architects Ictinus and Callicrates.

Work began in 447 BC and lasted nine years. Marble from Mount Pentelikón (16km or 10 miles northeast of the city), fa-

mous for its pure, milky-white grain, was quarried specially for the temple. It has acquired its present honey colour with the passage of time. Only the roof and doors were made of wood. The Parthenon is 70m long and 30m wide (228ft by 101ft). Its 46 exterior columns each rise 10m (34ft), and are constructed of about a dozen fluted marble drums placed one above the other.

The columns swell gently at the middle, leaning slightly inward, and the floor surface is convex. It is quite astonishing, but nowhere in the temple is there a straight line. One theo-

Pericles spared no expense in building the Parthenon, the city's most magnificent monument.

ry holds that this was designed to counteract the optical illusion by which straight lines, seen from a distance, appear to bend. All the subtly curving departures from both true vertical and horizontal give life and rhythmic movement to the stone. What's more – and this is the architectural stroke of genius – they give the structure a magnificent symmetry.

31

Aside from its cult functions, this supreme example of the Doric temple symbolized Athenian imperial glory as well as holding the national treasury. Ancient pagan temples were meant to be appreciated from the outside, so the Parthenon's altar, where live offerings were slaughtered, actually stood outside the building, positioned opposite the eastern façade. Only a handful of privileged persons – priests or high officials – were permitted to enter the sacred *cella* (inner temple).

Those admitted were able to view Phidias' masterpiece, the 12m (39ft) high statue depicting Athena Parthenos, Athena the Virgin, made of wood and

Masterpiece Mathematics

The harmony and power of classical Greek temples came not from inspiration alone, but from the application of the ancient principles of number and form, known as sacred geometry.

There were some definite rules: the height of a Doric column had to be 5½ times the diameter of its base; and that of an Ionic column 10½ times. Another key proportion in the Doric temple was 4:9. This is the ratio between the breadth and length of the Parthenon, between the shorter side and ceiling height of the inner precinct, and between the diameter of the 46 outer columns and the distance between any two of them.

The same ratio applied to the Propylaea which, if completed, would have been as wide as the Parthenon is long.

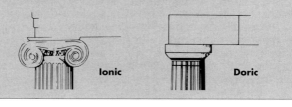

Ionic   Doric

covered with ivory and gold. The great ancient Greek historian Thucydides records its weight as 40 talents (1,052kg or 2,320lb), which was a conservative estimate. By the 4th century AD it had vanished forever, but you can see a 2nd century AD copy, the Varvakeion Athena, in the National Archaeological Museum – at 1/12 the original size.

The decoration of the Parthenon was arguably the most ambitious of any temple the world has seen, with sculptures at three levels. Little of this remains. The renowned 'Elgin Marbles' were removed by the British ambassador to Constantinople at the start of the 19th century with Turkish permission, and are now in the British Museum in London. Since then the Greek government has lobbied long and hard for their return.

Above the plain beam resting on the columns were 92 panels, each sculpted at 1.2m (4ft) square, called metopes, illustrating scenes of ancient conflict. Over the centuries most have been destroyed or removed (15 are in the British Museum). The best one that is still on show here is of a young Lapith, a mountain tribesman from Thessaly, struggling with a centaur.

Two massive triangular pediments, now virtually empty, crown the front and rear ends of the Parthenon. Once they were adorned with some 50 larger-than-life statues representing the legends of Athena. Although the building itself was largely left in its natural marble colour, archaeological evidence shows that the decorative elements were painted in vivid reds and blues.

During the 6th century AD, under Byzantine power, the Parthenon became the Church of Saint Sophia (Sophia, like Athena, means 'wisdom'). In 1205 AD, Frankish crusaders captured the Acropolis and turned it into a Catholic cathedral. Then the Turks, in the 15th century, used it first as a mosque (the Erechtheion was taken as the military commander's harem) and then as a munitions store, as which it was badly damaged by Venetian **33** shell fire in 1687 (see p.21). Restoration work on the Acropolis began after Greek independence in 1833, and has continued ever since.

THE ERECHTHEION (*Erechthíon*)

Across the Acropolis plateau at the northern wall stands the **Erechtheion**, a temple unlike any other in the ancient world. It originally housed three cults – those of Athena, Poseidon and Erechtheus – in one building. Constructed on irregular ground, the sharply different foundations contribute to its amalgamated shape. Built entirely in wartime, this was the last temple to go up on the Acropolis. Construction lasted 15 years, with the dedication being carried out in 406 BC.

This was the site of the legendary contest between Athena and Poseidon (see p.11). In a corner of the north porch you'll find an uncovered hole containing a rock with markings. According to some, these were made by Poseidon's trident; another version relates

that Zeus sent a lightning bolt down upon the scarred rock. There may have been an altar to the supreme god close by. As for Erechtheus, another of the part-man and part-snake kings of Athens, he somehow became so closely linked with Poseidon that they were worshipped together here as a kind of two-person deity.

Mythology aside, the north porch is considered a work of architectural genius. Note its dark-blue marble frieze, panelled ceiling and the bases and capitals of its columns.

Within the temple stood an ancient statue of Athena made of olivewood, which was said to have fallen from heaven. The saffron robe carried in the Panathenaic procession was draped on the idol at the end of the festival (see p.28), and a golden lamp burned perpetually before the statue.

The Erechtheion's familiar, much-imitated door, framed by rosettes, is found inside, between the two centre columns. One of the elegant side columns (each 7m or 22ft high) was taken to London by Lord

Elgin, who also removed part of the marble beam above. The capitals with palm-leaf patterns are especially elaborate.

The most famous feature of the Erechtheion, however, is the southern **Porch of the Caryatids**, where six proud, elegant maidens hold up the roof. Though named after a village near Sparta whose girls were noted in antiquity for their upright posture, the Caryatids were actually Athenians. The long tunics are draped in imitation of column flutings, while the fruit baskets on their heads replace capitals. The

The Porch of the Caryatids is one of antiquity's loveliest and most evocative monuments.

portico protected a holy place, the tomb of Athens' mythical founder-king, Cecrops.

Today's statues are replicas. Five of the originals were taken inside the Acropolis Museum after being damaged by pollution, the decay reaching 6mm (¼in) in depth. The sixth figure was removed by Lord Elgin to the British Museum.

THE ACROPOLIS MUSEUM

After you've admired the temples, visit the Acropolis Museum, sitting unobtrusively in a hollow at the southeast corner. Every exhibit in the cool interior was found on the site.

The first three galleries contain pre-classical works of the 6th century BC. Ancient Greek sculptors are admired as the first to portray the human form in a natural, though idealized way. They also produced some splendid animals. See, for example, the collection of **Four Horses** (570 BC) in room no. 2, especially the two in the centre with their heads turned shyly towards one another.

Also in this room is the outstanding **Moschophoros** – a marble statue of a man carrying a calf on his shoulders as a votive offering. Note the symmetry of the calf's legs and the man's arms, as well as the tension in his muscles and the detail of his hair.

In rooms 4 and 5 you have a chance to study the evolution **36** of the enigmatic smile and al-mond-shaped eyes that characterize the archaic period. The **Man on Horseback** (560 BC) is a fine example, even though the head is a copy (the Louvre has the original). Most of the statues in these rooms are *kore* (young women), which stood in the temples as handmaidens to the gods. **No. 679**, wearing a heavy shawl, or *peplos*, over her tunic, is superb. Most famous is **no. 674**, also known as the Almond-Eyed Kore. Dating from about 500 BC, this enchanting work captures the spiritual ideal in human form. After Persian invaders ran riot through the temple in 480 BC, this kore and other 'violated' statues were ritually buried by the Greeks, and lay undiscovered until 1885.

The head of the '**Blonde Youth**' (no. 689) (which was named after the yellow colour that once covered his hair) and the statue of the **Kritios Boy** (no. 698) are examples of the transitional stage from the archaic to the classical age of sculpture. Both originate from around 480 BC and show stirrings of individual personality.

Rooms 7 and 8 display parts of the **Parthenon frieze** and other fragments of sculpture. Watch for the splendid gods – Poseidon, Apollo and Artemis – awaiting the arrival of the Panathenaic procession. The relief of a winged goddess taking off her sandal (**no. 973**), from the temple of Athena Nike, illustrates the incredible skill with which Greek sculptors captured the relation between dress and the body.

The museum's final display is the original **Caryatids** from the Erechtheion (see p.34) – now safely protected behind glass and special lighting.

Before leaving the Acropolis, savour the view. The temple of Athena Nike faces west towards the Strait of Salamis. Far beyond that are the mountains of the Peloponnesus. To the left are the islands of the Saronic Gulf. Behind the violet shoulder of Hymettos to the east is Cape Soúnion. Below the south wall are bird's-eye views of the Odeon of Herodes Atticus and the Theatre of Dionysus, while all around is Athena's favoured city.

The Peploforos kore (530 BC), a handmaiden to the gods, was named for her shawl (above); the quadriga (570 BC) (below).

Ancient Athens

Ancient Athens, the city's historical heart, extends roughly from Syntagma Square to the Olympieion and, to the west, the ancient Agora and Acropolis. It also encompasses the old district of the Plaka (see p.45).

THREE HISTORIC HILLS

Three sacred hills lying west and southwest of the Acropolis guard the ancient city.

Areopagus (*Arios Págos*)

When you're herded out of the Acropolis at the end of the day, ascend the solid rock steps of the low hill nearby and watch the sun setting over antiquity.

Legend has it that here on the Areopagus, the god of war Ares was acquitted by a divine council of killing his daughter's lover (one of Poseidon's sons). According to Aeschylus' tragedy, this is also said to be where Orestes was judged to be not guilty of murdering his mother (see p.86) by the

Areopagus, or supreme court of ancient Athens. Originally, the court was made up of aristocratic archons (chief magistrates) who had been elected for life. With the development of democracy, however, their power was curtailed, but the court's reputation for integrity remained, and it continued to have jurisdiction over murder and religious offences.

Centuries later, in AD 54, St Paul preached on the Areopagus and made his first Athenian convert to Christianity.

The Pnyx (*Pníka*)

This terraced hillside is the location of the Acropolis Sound and Light performances (see p.105). The Pnyx – meaning 'tightly packed space' – is where the free citizens of 5th-century BC Athens met in democratic assembly. At that time, the rocky platform here was the site of the Stone of Vima, an ancient Speaker's Corner, where people gathered to hear the likes of Pericles, Themistocles and Demosthenes hold forth.

Filopappou Hill
(*Lófos Filopáppou*)

In ancient times, the site was dedicated to the Muses, and it's also called the **Mousíon**. The present name honours Antiochos Philopappos, a Syrian prince who served as Roman consul and Athens' benefactor in the 2nd century AD. The marble monument on the crest was erected in his memory. Once sacred, always strategic, this hill is an obligatory stop for camera enthusiasts: there's a superb view both of the Acropolis and Athens, sloping down to the Bay of Phaleron and Piraeus harbour. It also offers a peaceful respite from the noise of the city; there's a café halfway up the hill.

THE THEATRE OF DIONYSUS
(*Théatro Dionísou*)

The famous plays of Sophocles, Euripides, Aeschylus and Arisophanes were first staged here beneath the Acropolis, in what is now a rebuilt but crumbling theatre.

The original, 5th-century-BC theatre had seats hacked out of the earth around a circular stone dancing stage, flush with the ground. The semi-circular marble orchestra that you see today was sculpted by the Romans; the carved relief depicting scenes from Dionysus' life forms the façade of a raised stage. The backdrop of stone, *skené*, gave us the word *scene*. The theatre held about 17,000

The Temple of Olympian Zeus was – appropriately – the largest ever built in ancient Greece.

spectators. The names of top officials were carved into 67 front-row thrones of Pentelic marble. The place of honour is the lion-footed throne of the high priest of Dionysus Eleftherios. Just behind it stands the throne of Hadrian.

Before and after a play, Athenians would promenade

Summer plays and concerts are staged in the restored Odeon of Herodes Atticus.

in the **Stoa of Eumenes** (*Stoá Evménous*), an arched, two-tiered colonnade built in the 2nd century BC; only a section of it remains. It ran more than 150m (500ft) from the theatre along to the smaller **Odeon of Herodes Atticus**.

Atticus was a rich Athenian who donated the theatre to the city in AD 161, in memory of his deceased wife. The triple-tiered, arched façade is typical of Roman theatres, but the white marble seats are a modern restoration.

THE OLYMPIEION

South of the National Garden, the site of the Olympieion encompasses both Roman monuments and the ruins of ancient buildings that once lined the river Ilissos. The stream itself now runs underground through the city.

As was only fitting for the mighty ruler of the gods, the **Temple of Olympian Zeus** (*Stíles Olimpíou Diós*) was the largest in ancient Greece. It was begun in the 6th century BC by the tyrant Peisistratus, but was only finally completed by the Roman Emperor Hadrian in AD 132 (see p.20).

The temple included 104 Corinthian columns, each 17m (56ft) high and more than 2m (7ft) thick. Today only 15 remain, and there's no trace of the two gold and ivory statues installed by Hadrian: a giant one of Zeus and another, only *slightly* smaller, of himself.

To mark the separation of his own Athens – which he fondly called 'Hadrianopolis'

The Origins of Theatre

The origins of Greek drama are associated with Dionysus, the god of wine, revelry and inspiration. To celebrate the grape harvest, men and women would dance and sing around an altar, with the best dancers being awarded a goat, sacred to the god. The word 'tragedy' derives from *tragodoi*, meaning 'goat song'; *theatre* comes from the ancient Greek for 'to see'.

Over the years, poets recorded the songs of the chorus and added their own interpretations. The first recorded play was in 534 BC, with actors taking roles and speaking specific lines. As the art developed the actors, who were all men, wore expressive masks to indicate the age, sex and feelings of the characters. A crane-like device called a *mechane* was used to lower actor 'gods' onto the stage – the first special effects in history!

41

– from the ancient city of Theseus, a gateway – **Hadrian's Arch** (*Píli Adrianoú*) – was erected facing the temple.

A tip: whenever you see an arch, you can be sure that it is not classical Greek. The Romans invented the arch a few centuries later.

THE AGORA

While the Acropolis was the spiritual centre of ancient Athens, the Agora – sprawling beneath the northern walls – was the heart of daily life. Barbarian invaders razed the complex in the 3rd century AD, but as you wander through the rubble and foundations of the ancient marketplace, it takes only a little imagination to conjure up the shops, market stalls, state offices, law courts, mint, public archives, schools, library, gymnasium, concert hall, temples and altars of the old city centre, and hear the echoes of robed and sandalled citizens debating the issues of the day.

The Agora's spiritual legacy lives on: politics (as understood in the West) and philosophy (based on free and rational discussion) came into being on this very spot. Socrates held his famous dialogues here, at the shop of a shoemaker who, long before Plato, started to write down and publish a number of the sage's conversations. Later, Socrates' search for 'truth' fell foul of the authorities, and he was tried and condemned to death in 403 BC. Recent excavations have identified the prison cell in which he consumed the deadly potion of hemlock.

The huge gallery dominating the marketplace is a replica of the **Stoa of Attalos** (*Stoá Attálou*), built by the King of Pergamon about the middle of the 2nd century BC in homage to Athenian culture. It was rebuilt from attic marble and limestone in the 1950s by the American School of Classical Studies in Athens, the organization that has carried on the Agora excavations since 1931. Near to this 115m (382ft) long painted portico, or *stoá*, the philosopher Zeno founded the school of the Stoics. Here St Paul argued with the most sceptical audience he met in the course of his travels.

The museum within holds a large collection of pots, coins, household objects and pottery fragments (*óstraka*), on which the Athenians wrote names of prominent men they wanted to vote into exile (see p.15). Also here are a huge bronze shield taken from the Spartans during the Peloponnesian War and a *klirotírion*, an unusual device for relegating public duties by lot – an important feature of ancient Athenian democracy.

Classical Giants

Athens was the centre of art, philosophy and politics during the classical age. Among those who walked the Agora are:

Ictinus and **Callicrates**, architects of the Parthenon, and the sculptors **Phidias** and **Praxiteles**.

Two of the three great tragic poets were from Athens – **Aeschylus** (*Oresteia*) and **Sophocles** (*Oedipus Rex*). **Euripides** (*The Trojan Women*) was born on an island in the Strait of Salamis on the day of the great Persian defeat (see p.17). **Aristophanes** (*The Wasps, The Birds*), creator of Greek comedy, was also Athenian.

Herodotus, whose accounts of the conflict between Europe and Asia blended legend and fact, has been called the 'father of history'. Later **Thucydides**, (*History of the Peloponnesian War*), established an objective 'science' of history.

The philosopher-orator **Socrates** was seen almost daily in the Agora, earnestly engaging fellow citizens in dialogues on 'truth'. His student, **Plato**, recounted the master's teachings in *The Republic* and *Dialogues*. A political and religious philosopher, Plato founded the Academy, the world's first university. **Aristotle** studied at Plato's Academy before tutoring Alexander the Great in Macedonia. This renowned philosopher later established a rival school in Athens, the Lyceum (see p.52).

If you enter the Agora from the southern gate, down the hill from the Acropolis, you'll pass the pretty but anomalous Byzantine church, Agii Apostoli. From the entrance opposite on Adrianou Street (look for the pictorial reconstruction here that will help you visualize the original buildings), a path leads up a gentle hill to the first marble temple built by Pericles after the Persian wars.

The **Temple of Hephaistos** (*Naós Iféstou*) was devoted to the god of smiths. There were foundries and metal-workers' shops in this area in ancient times (similar outfits are still in action – across the railway tracks). It is more popularly known as the **Thisío**, because of the carved metopes on top of the columns, which show the expoits of Theseus. Other panels displayed here depict the labours of Hercules.

The Thisío is the best-preserved of all the temples in Athens, and measures around half the size of the Parthenon, with 34 Doric columns comprising its graceful peristyle. The aromatic garden that surrounds it is planted with various trees and shrubs, including pomegranate, myrtle, olive and cypress trees, which flourished there in Roman times.

If you return to the Agora's entrance from the Thisío, you will pass on your left the site of the Altar of the 12 Gods. In ancient Greece, distances from Athens were measured from this point.

KERAMIKOS

Lying to the west of the Agora, along Ermou Street, is the ancient cemetery Keramikós. Off the beaten tourist track, you can explore the extensive ruins and sculpted tombs in relative peace. This was the burial site of important Athenians, and the collection of rich jewellery, gold, glass and ceramics found in their graves, dating back to the 7th century BC, indicates their status. These items are on display in the cemetery's small museum, which with its strikingly beautiful painted vessels and unusual offering channels and figurines is a real gem for pottery lovers.

Plaka

Plaka, Athens' oldest quarter, is the most charming part of the city. Strictly speaking, the whole area south of Ermou Street is Plaka, but the heart lies close to the Acropolis. The two main thoroughfares are Kidathinéon and Adrianou, which intersect just below Platia Filikis Eterias, the quarter's large, leafy main square.

A mixture of ancient ruins, Byzantine churches and lively tavernas are packed into under half a square kilometre. The main delight here is the atmosphere of the winding streets, many of which follow ancient footpaths climbing up towards the Acropolis. Without warning you'll come upon stunning views of the Acropolis, the Agora, or the distant peak of Mount Lycabettus (*Likavittós*).

Plaka is drowsy and quiet in the heat of the day. The best

*P*laka's main square. Morning is the most peaceful time to relax here, in the shade of the trees.

45

time to visit is on a Sunday, when the Athenians stroll and chat with friends, and gather for long family lunches at their favourite tavernas. On any particular night, the cool breezes bring out Plaka's celebrated revelry: song and dance accompanied by *bouzoúki* music, spit-roasted *souvláki* and free-flowing *retsína* (see p.112). Restaurants, bars and souvenir shops are open late.

THE SIGHTS

At Kidathinéon 17 you'll find the very worthwhile **Museum of Greek Folk Art** (*Mousíon Laïkís Ellinikís Téchnis*). It houses fine specimens of embroidery, weaving, metalwork, wood-carving, ceramics, silverware, and paintings, and a broad collection of traditional costumes. What makes a visit to this museum so fascinating, however, are the detailed explanations of the traditions and craftwork that accompany the exhibits. The displays of jewellery, costumes and shadow theatre are particularly interesting. An annex of the muse-

um situated in the Old Mosque in Monastiráki Square holds a ceramics collection.

Continuing down Kidathinéon, turn left into Farmáki at the far end of the square. This route leads to the 12th-century church of **Agía Ekateríni** (St Catherine), which sits in a sunken courtyard. A couple of Ionic columns which jut up in front of the palm trees are believed to be the remains of a Roman bath.

Nearby, on the street of his name, the **Monument of Lysicrates** (*Mnimíon Lisikrátous*) dates from the 4th century BC. The six Corinthian columns support a dome built from a single block of marble. On top

The white-washed houses of Anafiótika are reminiscent of typical island villages (right).

stood a bronze tripod awarded to a boys' chorus in a drama competition staged in 334 BC. The frieze depicts Dionysus transforming Etruscan pirates into dolphins. In the 17th century, Capuchin monks incorporated the monument in their monastery (which later burned down). In 1810 Lord Byron stayed there and wrote poetry sitting between the columns.

Continue up Odós Tripódon with its impressive balconied villas from the early 19th century. In ancient times, winners of Dionysian contests placed their prizes – tripods filled with sacred oil – on pedestals along this street, whence its name, 'Street of the Tripods'.

Following Epichármou off to the left from Tripódon, you come to a remarkable white-washed village within the city: **Anafiótika**. To cope with the severe housing shortage experienced in Athens after Greek independence (see p.23), a law was passed which permitted anyone who built a house – or at least managed to get its roof up – between sunset and sunrise to occupy it. The first people to qualify were two stone masons from the tiny Aegean island of Anáfi. They were followed by other Anafiots, also masons, who built and restored houses and churches in their native style. As a result, this part of Athens resembles a Greek island, and today, the **47**

Anafiots living on the heights of Plaka outnumber the 350 residents on their native Anafi.

As you climb higher up in Anafiótika, the streets get narrower. Odós Pritaníou winds around to the top of the village at the base of the Acropolis wall, opening out to a spectacular view over Plaka. There's a more adventurous route, however, if you feel so inclined. A detour up Stratonos brings you to the enchanting sunken garden of a 17th-century church dedicated to the saints Cosmas and Damian, 3rd century Arab doctors who refused fees for their services. Turn right at the top and follow the labyrinthine white-washed path in between the houses – a hand-painted sign points to the Acropolis.

Walk down from here via Odós Erechtheós, where colourful tavernas nestle below the early Byzantine church of Agios Ioánnis Theológos, and then turn left on Lisiou, which leads to the lovely **Tower of the Winds** (*Aérides*), built by the astronomer Andronikos in the 1st century BC. It once contained an elaborate water clock that was fed by a spring on the Acropolis. Sculptures on each of the eight sides of the octagonal marble tower represent the eight points of the compass and the corresponding wind. You'll spot Notos, the south wind, pouring water from an urn, while Zephyros, the west wind, scatters spring flowers.

Spread out below the tower are the remains of the **Roman Forum** (*Romaïki Agorá*). On the far side, the four Doric columns were part of the Gate of Athená Archegétis, which marked the main entrance to the market area. One door support, protected by a rusty iron grille, is inscribed with Emperor Hadrian's edict taxing olive oil.

You'll also spot a **Turkish Mosque**, one of the two left standing in Athens from the days of the Ottoman occupation; it now houses an archaeology workshop. What's left of Hadrian's monumental library lies outside the Agora, at Adrianou and Aiolou.

Continue along Aiolou (also spelled Eolou), and turn left into Pandrósou, a 'flea market'

The delightful Tower of the Winds salutes the eight points of the compass.

of tourist shops selling leather bags, woven rugs, furs, slippers and worry beads. It leads down to the bustling **Monastiráki Square**, named after the Great Monastery founded here ten centuries ago, whose only remnant is the sunken church, the Pantánassa. On the south side of the square is the 18th-century **Mosque of the Turkish Bazaar**, which was built with marble from one of the massive columns of the temple of Olympian Zeus. Minus its minaret, it has now become a branch of the Greek Folk Art Museum. The first-floor balcony offers fine views of the market bustle below.

Weave your way around the vendors' carts selling cherries, bananas, coconut and pretzels to **Odós Iféstou**, which leads off from the metro station. The flea market continues along this street, which follows the exact course of an ancient path dedicated to the god of the smiths, Hephaestus; to this day it remains the centre for Athenian artisans who work with copper, bronze and iron. You can often hear and see them at work in the back of shops bedecked with copperware. Wander along the side lanes into Platia Avissinias, and you'll see wood-workers refinishing lovely old chests and chairs to sell at the antique stalls here. Monastiráki is always lively, but it's downright jammed on Sunday, when vendors from the region display their wares at the weekly sidewalk bazaar. **49**

CHURCHES

Retrace your steps along Pandrósou, which ends in the spacious Platía Mitropóleos. The **Mitrópolis**, Athens' cathedral, was completed in 1855 having been built from the remnants of over 70 demolished churches, including a zodiac calendar. On Good Friday evening, the famous candlelight procession takes place here.

The impressive interior, allegedly inspired by St Mark's in Venice, is bedecked with splendid marble pulpit, floor and columns, huge candelabra, and religious paintings shining with silver revetment. Every inch is covered in colourful geometric paintwork and mosaics. To the right of the entrance, a silver ossuary bears the sacred remains of Gregory V, the ecumenical patriarch of Constantinople; the ossuary on the left holds the relics of a 16th-century martyr.

The cathedral is open in the morning, and also from around 5pm to 7 or 8pm.

Beside the cathedral is the tiny and lovely **Agios Elefthérios**, the 'little Mitrópolis', which is affectionately known as Our Lady Quick-to-Answer-Prayers. It was built 800 years ago from much earlier columns and beams. Over the main door, a 4th-century BC pagan frieze has been nearly obliterated – stamped with the Latin cross by later Christians.

Kapnikaréa constitutes one of the best preserved Byzantine churches in the city.

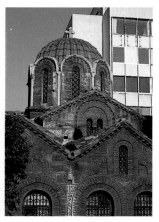

However, if you look carefully you can still see the wheels of the ship bearing Athena's robe in the Panathenaic procession (see p.28). This is all that's left of the only known artistic rendering of the famous ship.

Striking mosaics above the entrance to the cathedral glimmer in the setting sun.

Three more notable churches are nearby. The 11th-century **Kapnikaréa**, on Ermou, is one of Athens' best-preserved Byzantine churches. A modern master, Fotis Kondoglou, was responsible for the fine paintings inside.

Just around the corner on Aiolou, the city's older cathedral, **Agii Iríni**, has a blue-domed porch painted with the Star of Vergina, the venerable symbol of the Greek Macedonian people.

Sheltering under concrete columns at Mitropoleos and Pendelis, the tiny chapel of **Agia Dinamis** (meaning 'the strong') has held out against the modern office block built around it. Inside, faded frescos with silver and bronze revetment are painted on its walls. **51**

Modern Athens

Modern Athens extends from Syntagma Square to the north of Ermou Street. Of particular interest are Mount Lycabettus, the fashionable district of Kolonáki, and Omonia Square.

SYNTAGMA SQUARE

Ringed by banks, deluxe hotels, airline offices and travel agencies, Syntagma (Constitution) Square is the central reference point for most visitors to Athens. It also makes a convenient rendezvous spot for Athenians working in the city centre. Orange trees, cypresses and palms somehow survive the fumes that are emitted by constant traffic swinging into Syntagma from eight major thoroughfares.

Syntagma has always been an Athens centre of action: Aristotle's Lyceum was located just to the south; at different stages of World War II, the Germans and British had their headquarters on Syntagma; an unsuccessful assassination attempt on Winston Churchill occurred here in 1944 (dynamite had been planted in the sewers under his hotel).

Across the upper, east side of the square is Greece's **Parliament** (*Vouli*), which was the royal palace until 1935. Sentries (*évzones*) in traditional uniform guard a memorial to the nation's unknown soldier which stands in the forecourt. You can watch a formal changing of this Republican Guard at 10.45am on Sunday morning. Be advised, though, it's best to arrive early for a view.

Bronze shields on the marble retaining walls commemorate modern Greek military victories. There's also an engraved epitaph from Pericles' funeral oration (430 BC), honouring the Athenians killed in the first year of the Peloponnesian War. It's said ancient tombs lie underneath this site.

The Parliament Building occupies an upper corner of the sprawling **National Garden** (*Ethnikós Kípos*), an oasis of green in Athens' concrete forest. On Sunday morning, families and balloon sellers stroll the winding paths lined with

The gardens in front of the Záppion are a favourite summer strolling ground for Athenians.

exotic greenery and busts of modern poets. Peacocks, stray cats, a playground and a small zoo are among the attractions. To the south lies the **Záppion**, a national exhibition hall and, in summer, an open-air stage.

Nestling in the hollow of Arditos Hill (*Lófos Ardittoú*), the marble **Olympic Stadium** sits on the site of the stone original of 330 BC. This stadi-um, built for the first modern Olympics in 1896, holds no fewer than 70,000 people. It is just over 180m (600ft) or one *stadion* long, and is identical to the ancient U-shaped stadi-ums at Olympia and Delphi.

TO OMONIA SQUARE

Two broad avenues link Syntagma to Athens' other main square, Omonia (a 15-minute walk away). Along **Stadíou**, a principal shopping street, the **National Historical Museum** is in the old Parliament building on Platía Kolokotróni. Its displays from the Greek War **53** of Independence include the helmet and sword allegedly used by the poet Lord Byron.

Two blocks on is **Klafthmónos** (Sobbing Square), so-named because King Otto's subjects came here to register complaints. Just below the square is the lovely 12th-century Byzantine church of **Agii Theódori** (Saints Theodore), which has tiny stairs wrapped around a miniature pulpit.

Panepistimíou (also called Venizélou), with several 19th-century neoclassical buildings, runs parallel with Stadíou. The first building you'll pass is the former home of German archaeologist Heinrich Schliemann (1822-90), who found the ancient palace of Troy and unearthed the tombs at Mycenae. Up under the roof you'll see engraved 'Ilíou Mélathron' (Palace of Troy).

Further along you'll find the **Academy of Arts**, the **University** and the **National Library**. Their sculpted, gilded façades mimic the classical style. Athena and Apollo stand atop the Ionic columns at the Academy, while Socrates and Plato sit at the entrance. The Library has nearly a million books and manuscripts, including amazing hand-illuminated Gospels of the 10th and 11th centuries.

Both avenues converge on **Omónia Square**, a massive, roaring roundabout whose ra-

*F*ruit and vegetable stalls at the market offer a colourful view of daily life in Athens.

diating streets link the capital to its mainland provinces. Beneath its central fountains lie the central subway station and a shopping centre. Though the cafés and neon signs recall Piccadilly Circus or Times Square – only more grimy – Omónia, which means 'concord', is the most representative of all Athenian squares. It's a focal point for Greeks visiting from the countryside, and here life surges on in the streets and the *kafeneía* (coffee houses) with insouciant disregard for foreign tourists.

South of Omonia are the bustling **city markets**, where you can launch yourself into the pandemonium of Athinas Street, a chaotic bazaar which sells every plastic trinket and household gadget imaginable. Further along, colourful fruit, vegetable and herb markets border Sophocles and Euripides Streets; chickens, rabbits and wild game can be found on Armodiou; and huge, refrigerated, covered halls with long marble counters are home to the lively fish and meat markets along Aiolou and Athinas.

MOUNT LYCABETTUS AND KOLONAKI

Standing on Athens' highest point, at the summit of **Mount Lycabettus** (*Likavittós*), you enjoy a spectacular panorama of the city (marble maps on the terraces point out the main sights). A cable car runs up to the 277m (910ft) peak from Odos Ploutárchou in Kolonáki. Hearty climbers can make the trek on foot.

On Orthodox Easter eve, a candlelight procession makes its way up to Agios Geórgios, the 19th-century chapel which is perched at the top dedicated to St George. Cannons on the western slope are fired on Greek Independence Day and special occasions. The hill was never included within the ancient city walls; since it had no natural springs, it was untenable for any length of time.

The views from here are best early in the morning, before the heat and smog produce their inevitable haze. A visitors' pavilion provides refreshments, and there is also a modern amphitheatre nearby. **55**

To reach the cable car you'll pass through **Kolonáki**, one of Athens' most stylish quarters. The streets radiating off the main square, Platía Filikis Eterias (not to be confused with the one in the Plaka), are lined with designer shops and pleasant outdoor cafés.

Museums

NATIONAL ARCHAEOLOGICAL MUSEUM

The *Archeologikón Mousíon* holds more masterpieces of ancient art than anywhere else. Spanning perhaps 7,000 years, exhibits represent every period of ancient Greek history and every site unearthed from the world of the ancient Greeks. You will want to dedicate at least half a day to browsing through the fabulous treasury of sculpture, frescos, vases, jewellery, figurines, coins and everyday implements, and no matter how brief your tour, try to make sure that you don't miss the following highlights.

The **Mycenaean Room** (no. 4) holds the famous gold death mask of an Achaean king. It was recovered from the royal chamber tombs at Mycenae in 1876 by Heinrich Schliemann (see p.86), who was convinced it was that of Agamemnon, hero of the battle of Troy. In fact, the mask dates from the 16th century BC, at least three centuries earlier. Also look out for the 15th-century BC gold **Vaphio cups**, which depict the capture of wild bulls in a net, and the **silver libation vessel** in the shape of a bull's head, with gold horns and a rosette.

An adjoining room has important works of early **Cycladic sculpture** (2800-2300 BC), including a rare, standing male figure playing a double flute.

The museum's statuary rates universal acclaim. In rooms 7, 8, 11 and 13 you can see the progression of *kouroi* (standing male figures) through the archaic period to the superb **Kroisos** tomb statue of 520 BC. Amongst other marble highlights are **Phrasikleia** (540 BC) the Attic maiden, and the head of **Hygeia**, goddess of health,

MUSEUM HIGHLIGHTS

Acropolis Museum. Located on the Acropolis; tel. 323-6665. Open Mon 11am-6.30pm, Tues-Fri 8am-6.30pm, Sat-Sun 8.30am-2.30pm. Admission 1,500drs to site. Finds from the Acropolis hill, including many sculptures. Highlights include fragments of the Parthenon frieze and the Kore maidens. (See p.36)

Agora Museum. Inside the Stoa of Attalos; tel. 321-0185. Open 8.30am-2.45pm, closed Mon. Admission 800drs to site. Artifacts from the ancient marketplace and miniature models of the Acropolis and Agora in classical times. (See p.43)

Benáki Museum. Koumbari 1; tel. 361-1617. Re-opens in 1995 following renovation. Telephone for opening hours and admission. Ancient Greek and Byzantine art, jewellery, icons, costumes, silks and tapestries. (See p.60)

Byzantine Museum. Vas. Sofias 22; tel. 723-1570. Open 8.30am-3pm, closed Mon. Admission 500drs. Large collection of icons, panel paintings, Byzantine art and artifacts. Descriptions are given in Greek and French. (See p.60)

Cycladic and Ancient Greek Art. Neophytou Douka 4; tel. 724-9706. Open Mon, Wed, Thurs, Fri 10am-4pm; Sat 10am-3pm; closed Tues and Sun. Admission 250drs, free on Sat. Bronze Age artifacts and striking figurines from the Cyclades islands; also Greek art from Minoan to Roman times. (See p.60)

Greek Folk Art Museum. Kidathineon 17, Plaka; tel. 322-9031. Open 10am-2pm, closed Mon. Admission 400drs. A mixture of wood carvings, jewellery, embroideries, weaving, ceramics, paintings, silverware, traditional art and costumes from the Byzantine period to the present. (See p.46)

National Archaeological Museum. Patission 44, tel. 821-7717. Open Mon 12.30am-7pm, Tues-Fri 8am-7pm, Sat-Sun 8.30am-3pm. Admission 1,500drs. Marble and bronze statues, vases and archaeological treasures from prehistoric times to the Byzantine era, including the acclaimed Minoan frescoes from Santorini. The best museum of Greek artifacts. (See p.56)

The imposing bronze Jockey of Artemision was recovered from the sea after twenty centuries.

possibly by Praxiteles, which is considered one of the finest works in Greek sculpture.

Many of the ground-floor rooms are lined with marble *stele* – gravestones with relief sculpture depicting poignant farewells to the dead.

In room 15 you'll find the famous bronze of **Poseidon** (460 BC), standing poised to hurl his trident. It was dredged up out of the sea in 1928 by fishermen off the island of Euboea. The same men also discovered the bronze **Jockey of Artemision** (2nd century BC), urging on his branded steed, which is now on view in the Hall of the Stairs.

The **Youth from Antikythera** (340 BC), another outstanding bronze, can be seen in room no. 28. The figure is believed to represent Paris offering Aphrodite the prize apple, as it has been ascertained that his extended right hand once held a round object. Other notable bronzes include the **Head of a Philosopher** (3rd century BC) and the **Man from Delos** (100 BC).

At the top of the stairs is one of the museum's prime attractions: vivid **Minoan frescos** estimated to be 3,500 years old from the volcanic island of Thera (Santorini). A fisherman, boxing children, an antelope, and a spring landscape are among the graceful and sensitive portrayals of the great sea-going civilization of Crete. These frescos will one day be returned to the excavation site of Akrotiri, in keeping with the long-range plans of the Ministry of Culture to return some of the archaeological treasures to museums at their places of origin.

The upper floor houses an extensive **collection of vases**. Among the black-figure vases from the 6th century BC, watch for the famous jar showing Hercules fighting the centaur Nessos. The **Numismatic Museum**, with its coin collection, can also be found here.

The museum lies just 10 minutes from Omonia Square

Ceramic Styles

The decorative figures painted on Greek vases have been an important source of information about the ancient civilization and religion. The vase collection in the National Archaeological Museum dates from the first painted pottery of the Bronze Age (2000 BC) and displays an extensive range of styles.

Flora and fauna decorate the Creto-Mycenaean vases of 1700-1400 BC. Those of the Archaic period (1000-600 BC) are adorned with geometric patterns and sometimes animals. Black-figure vases were the predominant style from 600 to 480 BC; subjects from history or mythology were painted in black silhouettes on a red ochre background. These were replaced by the red-figure vases of the classical age (480-320 BC), when both mythological and festive scenes were painted in fine detail on a black or white background.

*E*arly armoured guns from World War I are on display outside the War Museum.

along 28 Oktovriou (Patission) Street. Descriptions are listed in English, French and German as well as Greek.

OTHER MAJOR MUSEUMS

The **Benáki Museum** (on Vasilissis Sofias and Koumbari Streets) features the handsome private collection of a wealthy Greek art lover in his family mansion. It includes ancient gold and silver jewellery, as well as Byzantine art, traditional Greek costumes, ceramics and icons.

Housed in a Florentine villa, the **Byzantine Museum** (Vas. Sofias 22) presents an impressive collection of icons, panel paintings and sculpture from the 9th to the 15th centuries. The religious artifacts – carved reliquary boxes, bronze and ivory pastoral staffs, gold-embroidered vestments, jewellery and silverware – are splendid.

The **Museum of Cycladic and Ancient Greek Art** (Neophytou Douka 4) is devoted to the Bronze Age art of the Cyclades Islands, and also has Greek works dating from Minoan to Roman times. The Cycladic marble figurines, which date from during the 3rd millennium BC, are a rare phenomenon in prehistoric art; yet the simple, minimalist features look strikingly modern. This rich collection was amassed by the Goulandris Foundation and is housed in a cool, modern building. Special exhibitions are also presented here.

The **National Gallery of Painting** (Vas. Konstantinou 50) houses a number of modern Greek paintings, much influenced by Byzantine and folk art traditions, as well as works by El Greco, Picasso and Utrillo.

War planes, early tanks and cannons are positioned around the **War Museum** (Vas. Sofias and Rizari Streets), which has battle gear from ancient times to World War II. The collection of guns, pistols, sabres, swords and armour – all highly decorative – is rather amazing.

Piraeus (*Pireéfs*)

Athens' port of Piraeus is the third-largest in the Mediterranean (after Marseilles and Genoa). With nearly a million inhabitants, upmarket marinas, pretty tavernas and a vibrant nightlife, it is a city in its own right, just as it has been since ancient times.

Today the world of seamen's cafés and 'ladies of the night' made famous in Melina Mercouri's *Never on Sunday* has been eclipsed by swish marble banks and shipping offices. Piraeus is no quaint fishing town, but a working port with busy streets radiating out from its three natural harbours.

The main port – or **Great Harbour** – serves international shipping vessels, cruise liners and the major inter-island ferries. From here you can catch the subway into central Athens, or wander through the colourful market behind the town hall. Many island people come just to shop in this boisterous bazaar, turn around and catch the next ferry home – without a nod at the rest of Piraeus or Athens over the hill.

Zéa Harbour, across the peninsula on the eastern shore, is peaceful and picturesque, with fishermen's caïques tying up next to sleek, luxury yachts.

Nearby, a spacious **Archaeological Museum** (Harilaou Tricoupi 31) displays the treasures of ancient shipwrecks around the harbours. The upper floor has three magnificent bronzes – Athena of Piraeus with owls and griffins on her helmet, a handsome Apollo, **61** and Artemis the huntress. In an adjoining room you'll find the marble remnants of the massive Kallithea monument.

Past the cafés along the Zéa marina, the entrance to the **Hellenic Maritime Museum** is marked by the black conning tower of a submarine. The museum traces the nauti-

*F*resh seafood, outdoor dining and harbour views are on offer at the harbour of Mikrolímano.

cal history of Greece from ancient times to the present and includes graphic displays of great naval battles. Remnants of the Long Wall fortifications built by Themistocles in the 5th century BC are incorporated in the building.

Further east lies **Mikrolímano** (which is also known as Tourkolímano), the third and most popular harbour. Its circular basin has a narrow exit designed for the sleek racing yachts that berth here. The quayside is lined with canvas-

covered outdoor restaurants serving up fresh seafood and a delightful view of bobbing masts and colourful pennants.

Kastélla Hill and the cliff-hugging road above Mikrolímano offer panoramic views of the harbour and the Athens area. You can reach Mikrolímano by taking the metro to the Néo Fáliro stop and then walking (about 30 minutes). The metro trip to Piraeus takes about 25 minutes from central Athens; you can also go by bus from Syntagma and Omonia Squares. Harbour-hopping is easiest by taxi, though drivers will charge you plenty for the privilege and claim 'port surcharges' when you protest.

Excursions

Athens is the gateway to the rest of Greece. With little more than a moment's notice, you can hop on a bus, a boat or a guided tour to visit some truly marvellous places, all easily reached on a half-day, full day or overnight excursion. Here is a sample of what's available.

DELPHI

The spiritual centre of ancient Greece, Delphi, sits in a stunningly beautiful setting on the slope of Mount Parnassus. According to legend, Zeus let loose two eagles from opposite ends of the earth. At the spot where they met he threw the Sacred Stone, marking Delphi as the centre of the world. Pilgrims journeyed from the farthest corners of the empire to consult the ancient oracle here, and during the 5th and 6th centuries BC, no important decisions of state could be taken without coming to Delphi first to seek its advice.

One-day coach trips to Delphi are popular, but it's strongly recommended that you stay overnight; otherwise you are unlikely to have time to visit all the sites. Also, the best time to appreciate the breathtaking beauty of the sanctuary and the scenery is at the end of the day (or early morning), when all the crowds have gone. You can go by public bus or rental car, or alternatively take one of the very informative tours run by **63** the major tour companies (see p.126 for further information).

Travelling northwest from Athens, you'll pass the city of **Thebes** (*Thíva*), which shows scant trace of its spectacular past. This was the city of King Cadmus and of Oedipus, who unwittingly married his mother after killing his father (as predicted by the Delphic Oracle). A gravel quarry along the road now occupies the spot where Oedipus met the Sphinx and answered the riddle.

Livadia, 119km (74 miles) from Athens, is a regional centre. It boasts a clock tower presented by Lord Elgin and a pretty Turkish bridge spanning the river. Roughly 23km (14 miles) west of town, you might make a detour to the monastery of **Osios Loukás**, a splendid example of 11th-century Byzantine architecture which has beautiful golden mosaics.

Beyond Livadia the road climbs into the Helikon range. At 2,500m (8,202ft), Mount Parnassos is its highest peak. You'll see beehives, herds of goats and low, stone shepherds' huts scattered over the stony pastureland – the region is known for its honey and *féta* cheese. In springtime the fields are carpeted with bright red poppies and Spanish broom.

Just outside Delphi is the lovely terraced mountain village of **Aráchova**, which is famous for its colourful *flokáti* rugs (see p.95), woven blankets and bags, and furs, as well as for red wine.

*S*hops at Aráchova village are a good place to buy textiles, including traditional flokáti rugs.

Hotels and Restaurants in Athens

PLAKA/SYNTAGMA SQUARE HOTELS

Esperia Palace
El Venizelou
Akadimias
Sekeri
Sadiou
Kolokotroni
Lakka
Diomias
Achilleas
NJV Meridien Athenes
Asthir Palace
Leoforos Vas Sofias
Diomia
Georgiou A
Ermbu
Grand Bretagne
SYNTAGMA
Mitropoleos
Imperial
Electra
Kamikareas
Plaka
Olympic Palace
NATIONAL GARDEN
N
Adrian
Aphrodite
Apollonos
Omiros
Voulis
Filelinon
Adrianou
Hermes
Electra Palace
Nikodimou
Amalia
Kednou
0   150 metres
0   150 yards
Nefeli
Adonis
Adrianou
Acropolis House
Xidathinaion
Leoforos Amalias
Thesbios
ACROPOLIS
Leoforos Vas Olgas

Recommended Hotels

All hotels are categorized by the National Tourist Organization (see Accommodation on p.116). Except for luxury-class establishments, prices in each category (from A down to E) must lie within certain limits, and rates must be posted in the rooms. However, prices are allowed to rise by as much as 20% in high season, and can drop by up to 40% in winter. All hotels listed here are 'C'-class or above. (AC = Air Conditioning.)

The more modest hotels might not accept credit card payment, and you may be asked to pay for the room in advance.

Prices quoted here are for a double room with bath in mid-season (ie: some places can be more expensive in high season). Most hotels also include continental breakfast in the rate.

▮▮▮	Above 21,000drs
▮▮	14,000-21,000drs
▮	Under 14,000drs

AROUND PLAKA/SYNTAGMA SQUARE

Achilleas ▮

Lekka 21, Syntagma Square
105 62 Athens
Tel. 323-3197, 322-582
Fax 324-1092

Bright and pleasant hotel set on a quiet street, one block from Syntagma Square and a few minutes walk from Plaka. Large rooms, most with sitting area and extra bed space for families. Rooms on upper floors have pretty garden terraces. Lounge, bar and breakfast room with central patio. Very good value. 34 rooms.

Acropolis House ▮

Kodrou 6-8, 105 58 Athens
Tel. 322-2344, 322-6241
Fax 324-4143

This restored 19th-century villa offers good-value accommodation with old-world charm, in a quiet corner of Plaka. 19 rooms.

Adonis ▮

Kodrou 3 and Voulis
105 58 Athens
Tel. 324-9737/8, 324-9741
Fax 323-1602

Newly constructed hotel pension in the heart of Plaka. Great views of the Acropolis and Mount Lycabettus from the roof garden. Parking facilities. 26 rooms.

Adrian   ‖

Adrianou 74, 105 56 Athens
Tel. 325-0454, 322-1553
Small hotel with roof garden. Balcony and bar. Closed November to February. AC. 22 rooms.

Amalia Hotel   ‖

Amalias 10
105 57 Athens
Tel. 323-7301/9; fax 323-8792
Comfortable hotel enjoying a central location, across from the National Garden. All rooms have colour TV, and there are a coffeeshop, restaurant, bar, and lounges. AC. 100 rooms.

Aphrodite Hotel   ‖

Apollonos 21
105 57 Athens
Tel. 323-4357/58/59
Fax 322-5244
Centrally located. Bar, central airconditioning. 84 rooms.

Asthir Palace   ‖‖‖

Corner Vas. Sophias Avenue
and Panepistimiou
Syntagma Square, 106 71 Athens
Tel. 364-3112; fax 364-2825
Luxury hotel located on Syntagma Square and offering Apokalypsis gourmet restaurant, bar and coffee shop. All rooms come with TV, video and audio system. 48 rooms, 30 suites.

Diomia Hotel   ‖

Diomias 5, 105 63 Athens
Tel. 323-8034; fax 324-8792
Average hotel set on a quiet street, near Syntagma Square and Plaka.

Electra Hotel   ‖‖‖

Ermou 5, 105 63 Athens
Tel. 322-3222; fax 322-0310
First-class hotel, centrally located close to Syntagma Square. Bar, restaurant. Bedrooms have soundproof windows, colour TV and mini-bar. AC. 110 rooms.

Electra Palace   ‖‖‖

Nikodimou 18
105 57 Athens
Tel. 324-1401; fax 324-1875
Pleasant hotel situated in Plaka district. Offering a rooftop garden and swimming pool with panoramic view. Restaurant, bar. Comfortable rooms, with colour TV and mini-bar. AC. Private garage. 106 rooms.

Grand Bretagne   ‖‖‖

Syntagma Square, 105 63 Athens
Tel. 323-0251/10; fax 322-8034
Traditional 19th-century British-style hotel, dating from 1862, with a marble-lined lobby, wood-panelled bar, and big, old-fashioned rooms. The 'GB' is an Athens institution. Three restaurants. AC. 394 rooms.

67

Hermes   I

Apollonos 19
105 57 Athens
Tel. 323-5514/6; fax 323-2073
A pleasant, modern hotel with attractive flower-covered balconies, set in a relatively quiet side street in Plaka, near Syntagma. Lounge, bar, restaurant, roof garden. AC. 45 rooms.

Imperial   II

Mitropoleos 46, 105 63 Athens
Tel. 322-7617/8
Average hotel situated on the edge of Plaka. 21 rooms.

Nefeli   I

Iperidou 16, 105 58 Athens
Tel. 322-8044/5
Small hotel occupying a position in central Plaka. 18 rooms.

NJV Meridien Athenes   III

Corner of Vas. Georgiou and
Stadiou, Syntagma Square
105 64 Athens
Tel. 325-5301/9; fax 323-5856
Offering luxurious rooms, fully air-conditioned and sound-proofed and complete with marble bathrooms and impressive neoclassical décor. Gourmet French restaurant. Conveniently located within walking distance of Plaka and Acropolis. Bar, 24-hour room service, TV and video. 183 rooms.

68

Olympic Palace   II

Filellinon 16
105 57 Athens
Tel. 323-7611, 323-7615
Fax 923-3317
Bar, restaurant, room service. AC. 90 rooms.

Omiros Hotel   I

Apollonos 15
105 57 Athens
Tel. 323-5486/7
Tourist class hotel offering roof garden, restaurant, snack bar. AC. 37 rooms.

Plaka   II

Kapnikareas and Mitropoleos 7
105 56 Athens
Tel. 322-2096/8; fax 322-2412
Good value accommodation set on the edge of Plaka. With bright, clean and quiet rooms, most of which have balconies – those at the back have a view to the Acropolis as well. Roof garden, café, bar. AC. 67 rooms.

SOUTH OF THE ACROPOLIS

Athens Gate   II

Vas. Syngrou 10
117 43 Athens
Tel. 923-8302/9; fax 325-2952
A Best Western hotel, located on a busy street across from the Temple

of Olympian Zeus. Roof garden, restaurant. 104 rooms.

Divani Palace Acropolis   ▯▯▯
Parthenonos 19-23
117 42 Athens
Tel. 922-9650/9; fax 921-4993
Good hotel in excellent situation, in a quiet street behind the Acropolis, just five minutes from Plaka. Offering a swimming pool, roof garden, bar and restaurants. AC. 253 rooms.

Herodion   ▯▯▯
Robertou Gali 4, 117 42 Athens
Tel. 923-6832/36; fax 923-5851
Plain but comfortable hotel tucked under the south side of the Acropolis, with rooftop bar, restaurant and cocktail lounge. Parking available. 90 rooms.

Ilissos   ▯
Vas. Kalirois 72, 117 41 Athens
Tel. 921-5371/922-3523
Offering bar, restaurant, cafeteria. room service. AC. 96 rooms.

Royal Olympic   ▯▯▯
Diakou 28-34
117 43 Athens
Tel. 922-6411, 922-0185
Fax 923-3317
Smaller than some luxury hotels, but with bar, restaurant, 24-hour

room service, beauty salon, swimming pool. AC. 297 rooms, suites.

AROUND OMONIA SQUARE

Aristides   ▯
Sokratous 50, 104 31 Athens
Tel. 522-3940, 522-3881
Plain, modern accommodation in a good, central location on Omonia Square, though it can be rather noisy. 90 rooms.

Athens Center Hotel   ▯
Sofokleous 26 (corner of
Klisthenous), 105 52 Athens
Tel. 524-8511; fax 524-8517
Situated south of Omonia Square, near the markets. Offering swimming pool, roof garden with bar, restaurant, private garage for parking. AC. 136 rooms.

Attalos   ▯
Athinas 29, 105 54 Athens
Tel. 321-2801/3; fax 324-3124
Set on a lively street in the market area. Roof-garden bar with view of the Acropolis. 80 rooms.

Candia   ▯
Deligiani 40, 104 38 Athens
Tel. 524-6112/7
Located opposite the main railway station, close to Omonia Square. With comfortable air-conditioned **69**

rooms, and good restaurant. Offering a swimming pool and a small roof garden. 142 rooms.

Delphi

Ag. Konstantinou 1
104 31 Athens
Tel. 523-8624
Old-fashioned hotel situated on a busy main road, but conveniently located five minutes from Omonia Square. 51 rooms.

Dorian Inn

Pireos 15-17
104 31 Athens
Tel. 523-9782
With swimming pool, roof garden, filling American buffet breakfast. Two bars and a restaurant, as well as room service. AC. 146 rooms, some suites.

Esperia Palace Hotel

Stadiou 22, 105 64 Athens
Tel. 323-8001/9; fax 323-8100
Restaurant, room service, snack bar and cafeteria. 185 rooms.

Keramikos

Keramikou 32, 104 36 Athens
Tel. 524-7631, 524-7082
Situated ten minutes west of Omonia Square. Rooms are small and plain but bright and clean, all with balconies and private bath. Bar and café. 30 rooms.

King Minos

Pireos 1, 105 52 Athens
Tel. 523-1111/18; fax 523-1361
Large, plush and centrally located, with restaurant and roof garden. In red light district. All rooms sound-proofed and air-conditioned. Parking facilities. 168 rooms.

Marathon

Karolou 23, 104 37 Athens
Tel. 523-1865/8; fax 523-1218
Pleasant tourist hotel on a busy street near Omonia Square. View of the Acropolis and Lycabettus. Roof garden, disco in summer, parking. 93 rooms.

Omonia

Omonia Square, 104 31 Athens.
Tel. 523-2710/20; fax 522-5779
Large, modern hotel set in a noisy but central location. Good value rooms with private bathroom and balcony. Rooms overlooking the square have a view of the Acropolis. 252 rooms.

Stanley

Odysseos 1-5, 104 37 Athens
Tel. 524-1611/18
Bright, spacious and comfortable hotel, used by package tourists. Awkward location if you're without transport, 15 minutes' walk west of Omonia Square. Rooftop pool with grand views. 400 rooms.

Titania ‖
Vas. Panepistimiou 52
106 78 Athens
Tel. 330-0111; fax 330-0700
Large, renovated hotel with comfortable rooms. Central location near Omonia Square, convenient to main sights. A large roof garden with panoramic views adjoins the piano bar. Good restaurant serving Greek specialities, 24-hour coffee shop. All rooms have colour TV and AC. Garage for parking. 400 rooms, suites.

AROUND MT LYCABETTUS

Alexandros ‖
Timoleontos Vassou Platia 8
115 21 Athens
Tel. 643-0464
Pleasant hotel occupying a quiet location at the foot of the Lycabettus Hill. Rooms are plain and modest, but clean, comfortable and spacious. Garage for parking. 96 rooms.

Lycabette ‖
Valaoritou 6, 106 71 Athens
Tel. 363-3514/8
This good value hotel is situated in Kolonaki at the foot of the Lycabettus Hill. There is no restaurant, but breakfast is served in your room. 39 rooms.

St George Lycabettus ‖‖‖
Kleomenous Platia 2, Dexameni
Kolonaki, 106 75 Athens
Tel. 729-0710/19; fax 729-0439
Luxury hotel in pleasant residential area, near Lycabettus Hill. No public transport. Pool, roof garden, bar, grill room with view of Acropolis. AC. 150 rooms, suites.

NORTH OF CITY CENTRE

Novotel Mirayia Athens ‖‖‖
Michail Voda 4-6
104 39 Athens
Tel. 825-0422; fax 883-7816
Large hotel used by business travellers. Parking, roof garden and pool. Sound-proofed. 195 rooms.

Park ‖‖‖
Vas. Alexandras 10
Piraeus, 106 82 Athens
Tel. 883-2711/19; fax 823-8420
Rooftop swimming pool, beauty salon, garage, 24-hour room service. Next to the Archaeological Museum. 145 rooms.

Zafolia ‖
Vas. Alexandras 87-89
114 74 Athens
Tel. 644-9012; fax 644-2042
Roof garden, swimming pool, private garage. 191 rooms.

71

EAST OF CITY CENTRE

Athens Hilton ||||
Vas. Sophias 46
106 76 Athens
Tel. 725-0201, 725-0301
Fax 725-3110
Huge – and with a splendid view of the Acropolis and the sea from the rooftop garden. With four bars and restaurants, business centre, health club, swimmimg pool. AC. 453 rooms, 24 suites.

Athens Holiday Inn ||||
Michalakopoulou 50
115 28 Athens
Tel. 724-8322/29; fax 724-8187
Easy access to centre. Bar, restaurant, disco, swimming pool, roof garden. AC. 188 rooms.

Athinais |
Vas. Sofias 99, 115 21 Athens
Tel. 643-1133, 644-1815
Fax 646-1682
Pleasant hotel located in a residential district about 3km (2 miles) northeast of the city centre. Roof garden. 84 rooms.

Divani Caravel ||||
Vas. Alexandrou 2
161 21 Kessariani, Athens
Tel. 725-3725/43; fax 723-6683
Easy access to Athens' business centre and the city's main sights.

Offering roof garden, three restaurants, indoor and outdoor swimming pools and three bars, as well as a 24-hour coffee shop. 470 rooms, some suites.

Golden Age ||
Michalakopoulou 57
115 28 Athens
Tel. 724-0861/9; fax 721-3965
Bar, restaurant, coffee shop, taverna. AC. 122 rooms, suites.

Ilissia |
Michalakopoulou 25
115 28 Athens
Tel. 724-4051/6; fax 523-7415
Set back from the road in a pleasant residential area. Parking facilities. 90 rooms.

SOUTH OF CITY CENTRE

Athenaeum Inter-Continental ||||
Vas. Syngrou 89-93
117 45 Athens
Tel. 902-3666; fax 921-7653
This huge luxury hotel is situated 3km (2 miles) south of the city-centre, and offers a rooftop bar and terrace, which enjoy spectacular views of the Acropolis. There is a swimming pool, two bars, four restaurants, a nightclub, TV, in-house movies, and a fitness centre. AC. 599 rooms.

Ledra Marriott |||

Vas. Syngrou 113-115
117 45 Athens
Tel. 934-7711; fax 935-8603
Excellent accommodation, complete with a Polynesian/Japanese restaurant and a rooftop swimming pool. Set away from centre, roughly 3km (2 miles) from the Acropolis. 256 rooms.

FURTHER AFIELD

Athens Chandris Hotel |||

Vas. Syngrou 385
Paleo Faliron, 175 64 Athens
Tel. 941-4824/6; fax 942-5082
This is a business/conference oriented hotel set in a coastal suburb, with a free shuttle service to Syntagma. Comfortable rooms and a pleasant lobby. Two restaurants, two bars, coffee shop, swimming pool, and parking. 350 rooms, 22 suites. AC.

Best Western Coral |

Vas. Possidonos 35
Paleo Faliron, 175 61 Athens
Tel. 981-6441; fax 983-1207
Occupying a pleasing waterfront location between the city and the airport, roughly 5km (3 miles) southwest of Athens centre, with balconies overlooking the Saronic Gulf. Offering roof garden, swimming pool, beach. 160 rooms.

DELPHI

Amalia Delphi |||

330 54 Delphi
Tel. 0265-82101; fax 0265-82290
Located on a mountain slope at the edge of town, enjoying views over the olive groves to the Bay of Itea. Restaurant, coffee-shop, lounges, swimming pool. 184 rooms.

Castalia ||

Vas. Pavlou and Friderikis 13
330 54 Delphi
Tel. 0265-82205/7
Situated on Delphi's main street, just 250m (820ft) from sanctuary. Central heating, restaurant with large veranda, scenic views, bar, lounge. 26 rooms.

Phivos & Phaethon |

Tel. 0265-82319, -82201, -82244
Two smaller, budget hotels, one on the main road, one up on the high road. Phivos has a good restaurant on the ground floor.

Vouzas |||

Vas. Pavlou, 330 54 Delphi
Tel. 0265-82232/34
Fax 0265-82033
Perched on a rocky ravine on the main street, close to the sanctuary. Offering restaurant, bar, lounges, large veranda with scenic views. 60 rooms, all with balcony.

73

Recommended Restaurants

In Athens, you can eat well in modest little tavernas at very reasonable prices, or enjoy a cosmopolitan dining scene at the many restaurants serving international cuisines. All eating establishments, except luxury ones, are price-controlled according to category. A service charge is included in the bill, but it's customary to leave a bit more. The following price guidelines are per person, and include a meal with wine and service.

▯▯▯	Above 8,000drs
▯▯	5,000-8,000drs
▯	Under 5,000drs

GREEK

Algebra ▯
Mouson 33, near Filothei
Tel. 692-5250
Taverna. Closed Sunday.

Apotsos ▯-▯▯
Panepistimiou 10
Tel. 363-7046
Marble-topped tables and wood panelling grace this typical taverna off Syntagma Square. Speciality is *bekri meze*. Closed Sunday.

Attalos ▯-▯▯
Erechtheos 16, Plaka
Tel. 325-0353
Excellent dining at pavement tables or at the flower-bedecked roof garden (beautiful views of the city and the Acropolis). Greek specialities and fresh seafood. Open until 1.30am; meals, drinks, ice-cream.

Bakaliarakia ▯
Kidathineon 41
Tel. 322-5048
This popular 19th-century basement taverna in Plaka claims to be the oldest in the city. It serves typical Greek fare, but is closed from July to September.

Blue Pine ▯
Tsaldari 37
Tel. 807-7745
Greek taverna in the Kifissia district, known for its world famous cheese and aubergine (eggplant) *bourekakia*. Other specialities include aubergine dumplings, curry. sweetbreads. Closed Sunday.

Brutus ▯
Voulgaroktonou 67
Tel. 363-6700
A quiet, pleasant taverna in the Kolonaki district.

The Cellar
Kidathineon 10
Tel. 322-4304
A colourful basement taverna in Plaka, popular with locals.

Corfu
Kriezotou 6
Tel. 361-3011
Traditional Greek cuisine, including some Corfiote specialities like *pastitsio* (minced lamb and macaroni pie). Centrally situated.

Delphi
Nikis 13
Tel. 323-4869
Centrally situated near Syntagma Square, popular for lunch and dinner. Wide range of Greek dishes and salads, omelettes and pasta.

Dionysos
Robertou Galli 43
Tel. 923-3182
A package-tour Greek restaurant with patisserie and outdoor dining – spectacular views of the Acropolis. Open round-the-clock.

Erato
Adrianou 134, Plaka
Tel. 324-7966
Named after one of the Muses, this friendly restaurant offers romantic dining in a vine-covered garden tucked away from the bus-

tle of Plaka. Good *mezes*, traditional Greek specialities and beautifully presented fish. Good-value set menu. Open day and night.

Everest
Tsakalof
No tel.
A Greek-style fast food restaurant serving pies, pastries, sandwiches and coffee, in the Kolonaki district at the corner of Odos Iraklitou.

Gerofinikas
Pindarou 10, Kolonaki
Tel. 362-2719
One of the city's grand old restaurants, it features Greek and 'Constantinople' specialities and fresh fish; a cosmopolitan atmosphere. Pleasant indoor courtyard.

Ideal
Panepistimiou 46
Tel. 330-2200
Pleasant and tastefully decorated restaurant serving unusual Greek specialities like *kokoretsi* (grilled lamb tripe) and international dishes. Closed Sunday.

Kafeneio
Epiharmou 1, Plaka
Tel. 324-6916
Specializes in *mezes*. Pavement tables. Closed Sunday. Other branch on Loukianou, Kolonaki.

Kentrikon

Kolokotroni and Voulis 3
Tel. 323-2482

A popular lunch rendezvous for local business people, with tables spilling out onto the terrace. Offering the usual Greek taverna menu and a variety of international dishes, with prompt and attentive service. Closed Sunday.

Kostoyiannis

Zaïmi 37
Tel. 821-2496

This is a huge, open air taverna which serves consistently good cheap food and is popular with students and travellers. The selection of main dishes includes tasty rabbit *stifado* (stew with onions), *souvlaki* with bacon, and quail. Closed Sunday.

Kouklis

Tripodon 14
Tel. 324-7605

This traditional *ouzeri* is always hopping and is popular with young Athenians and students alike. The menu is in Greek, but you won't need it as the day's selection of tasty *mezzedes* will be presented on a huge tray – just point to the dishes you want! *Ouzeris* serve *ouzo* – but red wine is also available. Good value, cheap and definitely cheerful.

Kyra Maria Tis Filotheis

Vas. Georgiou Chalandri 44
Tel. 681-5350

Typical taverna. Tables outdoors. Closed Tuesday.

Leonidas

Ano Varibopi
Tel. 807-9633

Taverna. Tables outdoors.

Loxandra

Sismanoglou 33, Vrilissia
Tel. 804-0192

Taverna. Tables outdoors. Closed Sunday.

Myrtia

Trivonianou 32-34, Mets
Tel. 924-7175, 902-3644

A large, well-known taverna offering a wide selection of *mezedes* (appetizers). Garden with strolling *bouzouki* players. In the Pangrati district. Closed Sunday.

Perix

Glykonos 14, Kolonaki
Tel. 723-6917

Specializes in *meze*.

Petrino

Corner of Themistokleous and Akadimias
Tel. 360-4100

Specializes in *meze* (large portions), and serves excellent Greek specialities and seafood in a quiet, pleasant atmosphere. The decoration includes plants, old advertising posters and photos of Greek movie stars. Closed Sunday.

Platanos   ▌

Diogenous 4, Plaka
Tel. 322-0666
Taverna. Closed Sunday.

Rodia   ▌-▌▌

Aristippou 44
Tel. 722-9883
An old-fashioned, romantic taverna at the foot of Mount Lycabettus. Closed Sunday.

Socrates' Prison   ▌

Mitseion 20, Makriyanni
Tel. 922-3434
Taverna serving popular home-made specialities. Outdoor tables. Closed Sunday.

Strofi   ▌▌

Roberto Galli 25
Tel. 921-4130
Traditional taverna with outdoor dining and a spectacular view of the Acropolis. Closed Sunday.

Themistokles   ▌

Vas. Georgiou B 31
Tel. 721-9553
Pleasant white-washed taverna in Pangrati district; a local landmark.

Xynou   ▌▌

Angelou Geronta 4
Tel. 322-1065
Traditional taverna in Plaka, very popular with local Athenian diners – reservations are recommended. Closed weekends and in July.

Dionysus-Zonar's   ▌▌-▌▌▌

Panepistimiou 9
Tel. 323-0336
Open round-the-clock, this is the best *zacharoplastio* (pastry shop and café) in the city. Other branches are located on Mount Philopappou and right at the summit of Lycabettus, both enjoying magnifient views of the Acropolis.

INTERNATIONAL

L'Abreuvoir   ▌▌

Xenokratous 51
Kolonáki
Tel. 722-9106
Specialities here include duck à l'orange and moules marinières (mussels), and there is an interesting wine cellar. Garden. Dinner served until 12.45am.

Balthazar   ▌▌▌

Tsocha 27
Tel. 644-1215
Fashionable international restaurant with attractive bar, in renovated mansion near the US Embassy.

77

Belle Helène   ‖
Palaiologou 1, Politia
Tel. 620-6427, 807-3659
Restaurant and bar with outdoor dining in pretty garden and open-air creperie. In the Kifissia district.

Boschetto   ‖‖
Alsos Evangelismou
Tel. 721-0893
One of Athens' smartest restaurants, specializing in the cuisine of northern Italy. Beautiful location in leafy Evangelismou Park. Dinner until 12.45am. Closed Sunday.

Brasserie des Arts   ‖‖
Meridien Hotel, Vas. Georgiou 2
Tel. 325-5301
Classic French specialities. Interesting wine cellar. Dinner served until 12.45am (last orders).

Buffalo Bill's   ‖
Kyprou 13, Glyfada
Tel. 894-3128
For those who like their meat thick. Dinner only Tuesday to Saturday; open Sunday from 2pm to midnight. Closed Monday.

Fatsio's   ‖
Efroniou 5, Pangrati
Tel. 721-7421
An attractive little restaurant serving Greek and Oriental specialities. Near the US Embassy.

Grand Chalet   ‖‖
Kokkinara 38, Politia
Tel. 808-4837
International cuisine with Greek specialities and live piano music, with a view to Mount Pentelikon. In the Kifissia district.

Je Reviens   ‖‖
Xenokratous 49, Kolonaki
Tel. 721-0535; 721-1174
Gourmet French and Greek cuisine. Enjoy the garden terrace in summer, or the traditional décor of the dining room with piano music.

Kona Kai   ‖‖
Ledra Marriot Hotel,
Vas. Syngrou 115
Tel. 934-7711
An unusual and popular Polynesian/Japanese restaurant with extravagant tropical décor.

Piccolo Mondo   ‖‖
Kifissias 217
Tel. 802-0437
French cuisine and piano music. Reservations essential. In the Kiffissia district. Closed Sunday.

Precieux Gastronomie   ‖‖
Akadimias 14
Tel. 360-8616
Chic, ethereal French restaurant. Lunch served until 4.30pm, dinner until 12.30am. Closed Sunday.

78

Stage Coach ‖

Kifissias 18, Maroussi
Tel. 684-6995.
Prime rib, T-bone steaks. Tables outdoors. Service until 12.30am. Closed Sunday.

Steak Room ‖

Aiginitou 6, Ilissia
Tel. 721-7445
Come here to try either a juicy steak or Wiener schnitzel at this international restaurant, situated not far from the Hilton.

Ta Nissia ‖‖‖

Athens Hilton, Vas. Sofias 46
Tel. 725-0201
A popular upmarket taverna-style restaurant serving a mixture of Greek and international cuisine. Open for dinner only, between 7.30pm and 12.30am.

Trattoria ‖

Farmaki 4, on Plaka's
main square
Plaka
Tel. 324-5474
Pizza, pasta and good Greek specialities are served at this friendly pizzeria and restaurant on the main square of Plaka. The outdoor tables are perfectly suited for people-watching, or alternatively you can dine inside if you prefer. Set menus are good value.

Vladimiros ‖‖-‖‖‖

Aristodimou 12
Tel. 721-7407
Enjoy charcoal-grilled lamb, veal, pork and beef in this restaurant's pine-fringed garden in the Kolonaki district. Dinner only.

SEAFOOD

Antonopoulos ‖

Friderikis 1, Glyfada
Tel. 894-5636
Seaside eating.

La Bouillabaisse ‖

Pentelikon Hotel
Diligianni 66
Tel. 808-0311
Enjoy great seafood and stay cool by the pool under the pine trees.

Dioskouri ‖‖‖

Dimitriou Vas. 16
Tel. 671-3997
Seafood and grilled dishes. Outdoor dining in the Neo Psychiko district. Dinner served until 1am. Closed Sunday.

Kanaris ‖‖‖

Mikrolimano, Piraeus
Tel. 412-2533; 417-5190
The best of many seafood restaurants in Piraeus. Dine beside the harbour, where your fish will have been landed fresh that morning.

79

Kranai Taverna   II-III
Mikrolimano, Piraeus
Tel. 417-0156
A large restaurant serving fresh
seafood along the harbour.

Mare Nostrum   III
Vas. Kifisias 292
near Psychico
Tel. 672-2891
Offering a good selection of sea-
food. Veranda. Closed Sunday.

Patiniotis   II
Pythagora 7, Castella
Tel. 412-6713
According to locals this is a good
place to come to try stuffed cuttle-
fish. Closed Sunday.

Psaropoulos   III
Kalamon 2, Glyfada Beach
Tel. 894-5677
A classic 60s restaurant, specializing in tasty grills and occupying a
pleasant waterside location not far
from Piraeus. Dinner is served up
until midnight.

Vaggeir   II
Koumoundourou 32
Mikrolimano, Piraeus
Tel. 412-2105
A friendly, family-run restaurant
at Mikrolimano, serving a good
selection of fresh fish in a water-
front setting.

VEGETARIAN

Eden   I
Lysiou and Mnissicleous 12
Plaka
Tel. 324-8858
You'll find vegetarian selections
elsewhere, but Eden is an all-vege-
tarian establishment – even classic
Greek dishes are adapted. Choose
between the pleasant, airy indoor
dining room and outdoor tables.
Dinner until midnight.

DELPHI

Phivos   I
Vas. Pavlou, Delphi
Tel. 0265-82319
Large, pleasant restaurant on the
main street, offering indoor dining
or a veranda with scenic views.
Greek specialities and omelettes,
as well as pasta, meat, poultry and
fish. Good-value set menus. Many
regional wines.

Taverna Vakchos   I
Apollonos 32, Delphi
Tel. 0265-82448
Mama supervises the kitchen at
this cheerful taverna serving low-
price Greek dishes. The large outdoor terrace has a great view of the
Bay of Itea. Breakfast, lunch and
dinner daily. On the upper road
next to the youth hostel.

The modern village of Delphi, Kastrí, is situated just a few minutes' walk from the ancient site. Perched above the Pleistos gorge, it offers stunning views across the valley, planted with four million olive trees, to the Bay of Itea, some 600m (2,000ft) below. There are lots of hotels, restaurants and souvenir shops, though advance booking in high season is a good idea.

Actually at the ancient site of Delphi, note the **Sanctuary of Apollo**, lying at the foot of two scarred crags called the Phaedriádes (shining rocks). Due to the bauxite which they contain, they acquire a rose-tinted glow at sunset. Emerging from the ravine between them is the **Kastalian Spring**, where everyone who came to consult the oracle could purify themselves with ritual bathing. If you're feeling repentant for any reason, you can still taste the waters here, and so cleanse your soul.

The Sacred Oracle

The origins of the Delphic oracle go back to prehistoric times, when the Mother Earth goddess, Gaia, was worshipped on this site. She and her daughters uttered prophecies from the Rock of the Sybil, which still stands within the sanctuary.

The Dorian invaders of the 12th century BC brought with them the new deities of the Olympian gods, who supplanted the earth goddess. Legend tells it that the god Apollo arrived in Delphi on a dolphin and slew the serpent Python, guardian of the sanctuary. In order to expiate himself for the blood he had shed, he then went into exile and worked as a slave before returning to claim the holy place as his own. Thus Apollo was seen to set an example of moral purity and a modest life for himself and mankind. Dionysus, the god of revelry, was also worshipped here, for the ancients believed a balance between prudence and pleasure made the perfect human being.

The Roman **agora**, where pilgrims bought supplies, precedes the entrance to the **Sacred Way**. As you mount the steps, imagine the holy path in its glory, lined with monumental bronze and marble statues and treasuries of gold and silver, as the city-states vied to offer the oracle the best gifts. Sitting at the bend in the road, the **Treasury of the Athenians** (507 BC) has been put together from its original, Parian marble remnants. Just past it you'll see the **Sybilline Rock**.

The path climbs sharply to Apollo's High Altar, where animals were sacrificed. Above it rise the commanding columns of the **Temple of Apollo**, dating from 330 BC (the temple of the classical age was destroyed by an earthquake in 373 BC). In the innermost shrine an aged priestess, the Pythia, was seated on a tripod. Suppliants believed Apollo himself spoke through the Pythia. Breathing intoxicating vapours from an underground chasm and chewing laurel leaves, she worked

herself into a frenzy, babbling incoherent phrases which the priests 'interpreted' in notably ambiguous hexameter verse.

Further up the mountainside is the **theatre**, built in the 4th century BC and enlarged by the Romans to seat 5,000. Higher still is the **stadium**, where the Pythian Games were staged every four years. It measures 178.35m (585ft), or one *stade*, in length. You can still see grooves for the runners' feet set in marble slabs at the starting block. Penalties for drunkenness are inscribed on the south wall.

The Delphi Museum

This museum houses some outstanding treasures from the sanctuary. Most famous is the 5th-century-BC bronze statue of the **Charioteer** (*Iníoches*). With a victor's diadem around his head and a look of calm pride, he is astonishingly lifelike. His eyes, which are made of white enamel and black onyx and are framed by tiny bronze wires for lashes, are preserved untouched.

*B*oth the Tholos (left) and the Bronze Charioteer (above) are renowned symbols of Delphi.

Other marvels not to miss are the 6th-century-BC **Sphinx of Naxos**, with the head of a woman, body of a lion, and wings of an eagle; the archaic *kouroi* of warriors from Argos, and fragments of the life-size **silver bull** that stood at the entrance to the Sacred Way.

Further along the main road, past the recent excavations of a gymnasium, you'll reach the **83**

Sanctuary of Athena Pronaia, also called Marmaria (the Marbles). This was the pilgrims' first stop on their way to the Oracle. Near the entrance are the ruins of one of the oldest temples to Athena, built about 650 BC; earlier remains of Mycenaean worship found here confirm its importance as a sacred place. The most commanding structure, however, is the **Tholos**, a marble rotunda which dates from 390 BC. Three of the 20 Doric columns which encircled an inner shrine have been reconstructed and topped with their entablature. Though similar buildings stood at Epidaurus and Olympia, the purpose of the Tholos is still unknown.

DAPHNI AND ELEUSIS

It's worth putting up with the 10km (6 miles) of dreary scenery from the centre of Athens to reach the 11th-century Byzantine monastery at Daphni (Dafní), celebrated for its mosaics. Two enormous cypresses and an olive tree mark the entrance in a tall wall.

Nothing in Western art will prepare you for the stupendous **Christ Pantocrator** in the dome – to be viewed, as the artists intended, from the entrance. The other mosaics in the church are also worth lingering over (binoculars help in studying details). Look particularly for the one depicting the crucifixion, with its moving portrayal of the Virgin Mary's grief. Though the monastery is no longer inhabited, an autumn wine festival is held in the grounds.

As you proceed on the main Corinth road past heavy industry and oil refineries, you'll probably find it hard to imagine that this was Attica's most fertile area in classical times. Go past Skaramangás with its enormous shipyards, and continue on to **Elefsína** (22km or 13 miles from Athens), site of the temple of the earth goddess Demeter, and the ruins of the former cult centre of the Mysteries of Eleusis.

At least 3,500 years ago, Eleusis was a sacred shrine, and not until AD 395, when the pagan gods were banned, did the sanctuary lose its significance. The Mysteries were remembered every year with a major procession along the Sacred Way between Eleusis and the Athens Acropolis. Secrecy shrouded the Mysteries, but it is thought that initiates had to swear not to reveal the secrets of fertility and life after death. Aeschylus, the tragedian from Eleusis (525-456 BC), was just about executed when it was suspected that he had given away some of the Mysteries in one of his plays.

Despite its industrial surroundings, the Eleusis Museum is worth a visit.

THE CORINTH CANAL AND THE ARGOLID

It is said that the Roman Emperor Nero was the first person to attempt to realize the ancient dream of connecting the Saronic and Corinthian gulfs. He started the digging in AD 67 when he ceremoniously dug out the first pile of earth with a golden shovel. In those days, the ships were winched and dragged across the narrow isthmus – a system preferred to the perilous journey around the storm-lashed southern cape of the Peloponnesian peninsula. It was only in 1882, however, that digging started in earnest, and eleven years later, the gulfs were linked by the **Corinth Canal**, almost 6.5km (4 miles) long but only 25m (82ft) wide and 8m (26ft) deep. Only one ship can pass through at a time.

The completion of the Corinth Canal in 1893 marked the realization of an ancient dream.

The **Argolid** – the eastern peninsula which juts into the Saronic Gulf – constituted the heart of Greece in Mycenaean times (1600 BC to 1100 BC). Blazingly hot in summer, it is a region of orange and lemon groves, where small ceramic and bronze workshops flourish in the villages.

High above the plain, the imposing acropolis of **Mycenae** (*Mikínes*) was the richest and most sovereign power of its day. Agamemnon marched from here to lead the Greeks to victory against Troy. The citadel was built between 1350 BC and 1200 BC. The ramparts of massive, rough-hewn blocks are known as the **Cyclopean walls**, since the ancient Greeks could not conceive of anyone but the gods' one-eyed giants being able to move them into place. Within them the Mycenaean kings heaped the gold, jewels and rich spoils from their extended wars.

The entrance to the fortress is through the awesome **Lion Gate**, the earliest known mon-

The Curse of the House of Atreus

Mycenae is haunted by the dark tragedy of the house of Atreus, as told by the poet Aeschylus in his trilogy, the *Oresteia*. Caught up in a bitter rivalry for the rule of Mycenae, Thyestes placed a curse on his brother, King Atreus, and all his progeny. Before leaving to fight in the Trojan War, Atreus's son, Agamemnon, sacrificed his daughter, Iphigenia, to gain favourable winds for his journey. Upon his return his vengeful wife, Clytemnestra, led him to a warm bath where her lover, Aegisthus, lay in wait to kill him with a dagger.

Agamemnon's son, Orestes, escaped, but later returned to avenge his father's death by slaying his mother and her lover. He was then haunted by the Furies, who stung him with guilt and anguish until he was pardoned by Athena.

umental sculpture in Europe. The heads of the beasts were never found, but it is thought they were made of gold. Inside the gate, to the right, is **Grave Circle A**, excavated by Schliemann in 1876. In the six royal shaft graves (family mausoleums enclosed in the circular stone parapet) he discovered 19 skeletons and 14kg (30lb) of gold. The treasures are now in the National Archaeological Museum in Athens (see p.56).

You can climb up the rocky slope to explore the palace and throne room. Outside the fortress and below the Lion Gate near Grave Circle B, are two of the monumental **beehive tombs** – tall, vaulted burial chambers which were dug into the hillside. Due to the amplified acoustics, even the lightest footsteps sound like a marching army. Further down the road is the greatest of the beehive tombs, measuring 13.4m (44ft) high and 14.6m (48ft) in diameter, which is known as the **Treasury of Atreus**.

The other major site of the region is the **Theatre of Epidaurus** (*Epídavros*). Built in

*T*he tall beehive tombs at Mycenae are just some of the site's Bronze Age wonders.

the 4th century BC, it is the best preserved of all the ancient theatres in Greece. The limestone benches sat 12,000 spectators, and the acoustics are so perfect that if you stand at the top you really *can* hear a pin drop down in the orchestra. Greek drama is still performed here every summer.

*A*ccoustics at the Theatre of Epidaurus are so perfect that you can hear a pin drop.

In its day, the theatre was merely an adjunct to the **Sanctuary of Asklepios**, one of the most important healing centres of ancient times. You can wander among the ruins, which lie in a sweet-smelling meadow surrounded by cypress trees; the serenity of the site means it still feels like a place of healing. The little museum shows sculpture from the temples.

Nafplio, or Nauplia, makes a pleasant base for exploring the surrounding region. Overlooking a large bay, the town is a picturesque mix of neoclassical and Venetian-style houses, Turkish fountains, waterfront restaurants and mosques. A well-preserved Venetian fort towers above the town, which offers two good museums.

An extended sojourn here would allow you to take in the Bronze-Age palace at **Tiryns**, which also boasts awesome cyclopean walls; the interesting archaeological museum at **Argos**, and other minor ruins in the area. If time is limited, you can see the Corinth Canal, Mycenae and Epidaurus on a one-day coach tour.

SOÚNION

This windswept promontory lies 70km (43 miles) south of Athens and is crowned by the **Temple of Poseidon**. From this southernmost point on the mainland you can see the Saronic Gulf, the Aegean Sea, several islands and what is arguably the most beautiful sunset or sunrise in Attica.

The temple was built of Parian marble around 444 BC. Of its original 34 Doric columns, only 15 still stand – Lord Byron carved his name on one of them – while the salty sea wind has eaten away at the Ionic frieze depicting mythical battles. There's a beach resort on the shore, below one side of the precipice; on the other is a sheer 60m (197ft) drop.

This is a popular excursion from Athens and takes from 1½ to 2½ hours each way, depending on the traffic. Along the winding coastal highway you'll find good, sandy beach-es (see p.118) and spectacular seascapes, especially over the last 12km (7 miles). You can go by local bus, rented car or organized tour. Unless you opt for the latter, the best times to visit are sunrise and sunset. If you can avoid the afternoon hours when the tour buses descend, you may feel a sense of the inspiration that moved Lord Byron to write:

Place me on Sunium's marbled steep,
Where nothing, save the waves and I,
May hear our mutual murmurs sweep;
There, swan like, let me sing and die.

THE SARONIC ISLANDS

On even the briefest Athens holiday, you can have a taste of the island life and the open sea. The islands of the Saronic Gulf are only a couple of hours away from the Greek capital. Three of them – Aegina, Poros and Hydra – can be visited on a one-day cruise; ask at any travel agency or your hotel. A **89**

*C*ape Soúnion offers lovely views of the island-dotted waters of the Saronic Gulf.

daily ferry and hydrofoil service (see p. 136) make it easy – not to mention considerably cheaper – to go on your own. You can expect crowds on summer weekends, as the Saronic Islands are a favourite playground for Athenians escaping the city heat.

Note: It's breezy on deck and squalls may occur. Take a jacket or sweater along.

Aegina (*Égina*)

Aegina, situated 1¼ hours from Piraeus, is famed for its pistachio nuts, ceramics and local wine. It also boasts the well-preserved Temple of Aphaia, dating from the 5th century BC.

The main port of Aegina Town offers a bustling, quayside scene. South of the capital you'll find the seaside village

of Marathon, followed by the fishing port of Perdika, 9km (5½ miles) away. There's a superb beach here, but it may be crowded, as many Athenians have summer houses on this island. Small boats ferry visitors out to the pretty islets of Angistri and Moni, where you may find a bit of solitude.

The resort complex of Agia Marina, 15km (9 miles) from Aegina, has a long, sandy (and crowded) beach, water-skiing, mini-golf and a boat basin. The temple is nearby.

The Tragedy of King Aegeus

According to legend, every nine years it was an obligation of the Athenians to send seven youths and seven maidens to Crete to be eaten by the dreaded Minotaur. Theseus set out for the island on a ship with black sails to slay the monster, while his father, King Aegeus, gazed upon the sea, watching for his son's return. If Theseus escaped alive, he was to hoist the white sails of victory for his father to see.

With his mission successfully accomplished, Theseus sailed back to Athens, but in his euphoria forgot to change the sails. So it was that when the black sails of death came into sight, the grief-stricken king, believing his son to be dead, threw himself off the precipice at Soúnion, and the sea was thereafter called the Aegean.

Póros

The ferry approach to Póros – through the extremely narrow channel that separates this pine-covered island from the Peloponnese – is serenely beautiful. The charming port town climbs up the sides of a small hill, sporting the typical island architecture of white walls and blue woodwork. The long waterfront promenade is lined with fishing caïques and is a colourful place to inspect the day's catch.

This is also a popular summer resort, and offers splendid yachting, snorkelling, fishing and water-skiing. There are many secluded coves within walking distance of the town, and a longer but pleasant hike (5km/3 miles) will bring you to the remains of a temple to Poseidon where Demosthenes, the famous Athenian orator, committed suicide rather than surrender to one of Alexander the Great's generals in 322 BC.

Póros lies 2½ hours by ferry from Athens, and 1¼ hours from Aegina.

Hydra (Ídra)

This is a barren, rocky island turned cosmopolitan artists' colony – the Greek answer to Capri or St Tropez. Its spectacular harbour remains hidden

The pretty town of Hydra – where there are no roads and no cars, but plenty of donkeys.

from sea view until just before you enter the port. Then, as if a curtain had suddenly risen, Hydra Town appears. Its cluster of Italianate villas rises majestically up the slopes above glittering masts and dazzling sails. There are no roads and no cars, but many donkeys.

In lieu of sandy beaches, swimming is best off shaved rocks (the clarity of the water is memorable). Outside town, the island is extremely bare, though you can always hire a small boat to take you along the north shore, where you'll find occasional shade. Monasteries and churches dot the rugged slopes. Most visitors simply stick to the port, however, where they browse in the boutiques and art galleries, or watch the 'beautiful people' going about their holidays.

Hydra can be reached by a regular ferry service which runs from Athens. The journey time is 3 to 4 hours, which still leaves you enough time to explore the pretty town and have a leisurely lunch or a swim before catching one of the late boats back.

Spétses

Spétses, last of the string of main islands in the Argosaronic region, is wooded, hilly and dotted with stately mansions. With few motor vehicles, most transport is by bicycle or donkey carriage. Beaches – some sandy, some rocky – are less crowded than the other islands and there is a lot of after-dark entertainment on offer.

Spétses is a 4-5 hour trip by regular ferry from Athens, or faster by hydrofoil.

93

What to Do

Shopping

For luxury shopping, the best buys are in carpets, furs, jewellery, embroidery, folk art and icons. Always shop around before you buy, since prices and quality vary widely from one shop to the next. Feel free to ask questions, handle anything you're interested in, turn it upside down (and, if it's clothing or needlework, inside out as well!). Your best bet is to stick to handmade items. Labour is still cheap here, and the quality of rural and island handicrafts high. Incidentally, if you buy something too big to carry, Greek commercial enterprises are adept at mailing abroad.

Athens' best and most expensive shops are located in **Kolonáki** and around **Syntagma Square**, while **Omonia Square** offers cheaper shops. For women's fashions, try the stores along **Ermou Street**; for statues, jewellery, sponges and all kinds of souvenirs, stroll down **Pandrossou** and **Adrianou Streets** in Plaka.

Go to **Monastiráki** for copper and brass, kebab skewers, leather bags, goat bells, handmade *bouzoúkis*, daggers in decorative scabbards, and worry beads (*kombolóïa*). Keep an eye open for items made from olive wood – salad bowls in particular. You'll find antique dealers in this area, too – beautiful wooden chests at the furniture stalls – while the daily flea market is the place to hunt for original, hand-crafted work from all over Greece.

BARGAINING

Bargaining is common practice in Athens, except at department stores, food shops or the fashionable clothes shops. Most stores will offer you a 'better price' than that which is marked, and with a little bargaining you may get it for even less, especially if you use cash and not a credit card. (Certain places are delighted to accept your hard currency.) In Monastiráki, be prepared to haggle – it's part of the game. A winning smile and a relaxed, un-hurried attitude will usually do wonders – just make sure that you are not talked into buying something you don't want.

WHAT TO BUY

Rugs, carpets and needle-point: *flokáti* rugs (priced by the kilo – 1sq metre weighs about 2½kg or 5½lb) come ei-ther machine-made or, prefer-ably, hand-woven. Made from pure sheep's wool shag, they are spun from fibres into yarn

and then looped together to be processed under water. These rugs should be hand-dyed with natural dyes in solid colours. Prices vary, so shop around. You can find some good buys in Athens, and also in Arácho-va, on the way to Delphi.

Many shops sell beautiful woven rugs and carpets, in ad-dition to smaller embroidered

Keep an eye open for good buys, especially woven rugs, car-pets and needlework items.

cushion covers and wall hangings. The needlepoint tradition is slowly dying out, so the genuine, hand-sewn article will always be a wise buy. One way to tell if the work is hand-done is to examine the back of the item. Have a look at the stitches – if they are uniform, it's probably been machine-sewn; handwork will sport a hodge-podge of knots and threads. Two shops to try are Village Flokáti, Mitropoleos 19, and Midas, Pandrosou 7-15.

Furs: furs have long been a thriving industry here, and you will see fur coats, stoles, capes and hats – often dyed in garish colours – on display throughout Athens. These can be a good bargain, if they're what you like. The secret of the pelt-strip coat lies in the sewing, which varies in quality. Shop carefully, ask questions and resist the hard sell in fur shops until you've found out whether the sewing is completely hand-done and verified both the origin and quality of the pelt (as some come from Far Eastern fur-farms, not Greek villages).

Jewellery: reproductions of museum jewellery in gold and silver are definitely worth a second look. Consider copies of the Byzantine jewellery on sale in the Benáki Museum. The other major museums also have gift shops selling quality reproductions of jewellery, silverware and sculpture. Many offer good buys.

For the best jewellery shops look around the Voukourestíou and Panepistimíou area. Gold and silver are sold by weight; each item should be weighed in front of you. Workmanship and creativity involve an additional cost. Some gold rings are made from two different purities; check for hollowness and the correct weight-price equivalents. Enamel cannot be graded for quality, so be wary about anything which seems too spectacular.

Icons and folk art: before you purchase any handicrafts, visit the **National Organization of Hellenic Handicrafts**, which is at Mitropoleos 9. The goods here are not for sale, but by checking the items displayed you'll get a good idea of standards of quality and price.

Another place to try is the **National Welfare Organization**, which sells copperware, embroidered silks for framing (*tsevrédes*), rugs, carpets, ceramics and a variety of other genuine Greek handicrafts. All merchandise has been meticulously inspected by the authorities, and the profits go to a worthwhile cause. This is one place where you can't bargain, but prices are very reasonable. There are two locations: Ipatias and Apollonos Streets in Plaka, and Vas. Sophias 135 in Ambelokipi.

Buying **icons** can be a tricky business. Make sure you find a reputable dealer who doesn't sell poor copies. Warped and cracked wood may not necessarily mean that a piece is old or Byzantine. These religious images can be modest, indeed humble. All icons should have some degree of spirituality and as a rule this doesn't come out of a backroom assembly line. Note that you must have government permission to export authentic originals and that

icon smuggling is a jailable offence in Greece.

The streets off the cathedral square sell a plethora of Orthodox **furnishings**. Some antique shops display *támata*, the silver votive offerings which you will see attached to church icons. They're mainly aluminium now, but are still fashioned in the shape of body parts. Origins of this practice date back to ancient times.

Y*ou'll come across many shops selling replicas of icons and other religious artifacts.*

Sports

WATERSPORTS

Swimming. A number of hotels around town have **pools**, which non-residents may use for a fee. In Piraeus you won't want to go in the sea, but at the Zéa yacht marina (see p.61) there is an attractive, Olympic-size, salt-water pool, a restaurant and excellent facilities. A fee is charged for admission, and children under eight are not allowed in.

Clean, sandy **beaches** are easily reached by bus, taxi or car from the centre of Athens. Obviously, the further you go from the city, the clearer the air and the cleaner the water (see p.118). For the nearest good sea bathing, head along the Attica coast towards Soúnion. Buses 116 and 117 leave from Vas. Olgas Avenue, opposite the main entrance to the temple of Olympian Zeus, and go as far as Várkiza (32km/20 miles from Athens). For Soúnion and other points beyond Várkiza take a bus from Mav-

romatéon Street, just past the Archaeological Museum. The tourist office has timetables.

You will find the following recreational spots on the way to Soúnion from Athens:

Aghios Kosmas (tel. 781-5572) is an athletic complex located across from the West Terminal of Athens Airport. It has tennis courts, soccer fields, running tracks, and basketball and volleyball courts. An organized beach and three heated, open-air, Olympic-size swimming pools are nearby.

Glyfáda (12km or 7 miles from Athens) is a famous summer resort, with sandy beaches, a marina and good hotels. **Astír Beach** (tel. 806-0202) is an organized swimming area amid pine and olive trees, operated by the National Tourist Organization (EOT), complete with snack bars, a restaurant and very expensive bungalows for hire. A major drawback is the noise of the jets from nearby Athens airport.

Voúla (20km/12 miles from Athens; tel. 895-1646) has another EOT beach, less luxurious but well run and with a lovely view over the bay. It's also much quieter.

The resort of **Vouliagméni** (tel. 896-0906), situated 5km (3 miles) further south, is a more upmarket place, with a yacht club and deluxe hotel complex. Also here is a public beach with water-skiing facilities, and you can charter a fishing caïque at the marina. The town is named after a sulphur-springs lake, which has been converted into a spa (tel. 896-0341), where the warm, lime-coloured waters are supposed to be good for muscular aches and skin ailments.

Between the lake and Várkiza you'll find parking niches dotted along the highway from where you can climb down to the scores of rocky covelets which decorate the coastline. This coastal stretch is not recommended for either children

Inter-island cruises are a good way to explore the islands and beaches of the Saronic Gulf.

or poor swimmers, but the lovely beach at **Várkiza** (tel. 897-2102), with its pistachio trees growing almost to the shore, is perfectly safe.

More beaches still technically on the Saronic Gulf can be found at **Lagonísi, Saronís** and **Anávissos**. You'll start to feel the open Aegean as you approach the delightful beach and tavernas at **Soúnion**.

Like most of Attica, the area which is located inland between Athens and Soúnion is very dry, and you should be particularly careful here with matches and cigarette butts. In summer, the wind can turn the tiniest spark into a roaring inferno in a matter of minutes.

For less developed and less crowded beaches, head along the **Marathón coast** of eastern Attica. Buses leave from Mavromatéon Street and take about an hour to the area of the famous battlefield. Along the coastline you'll find numerous seafood tavernas. Other buses run to Néa Mákri and Agios Andréas, or alternatively you can take a ferry from Rafína to the island of Euboea (Évia).

Sailing: sailing clubs throughout the country organize international regattas every year. For more information try the Sailing Federation, Navarhou Koundourioti 7, Castela, Piraeus; tel. 413-7351.

Yacht Charters: cruising the Aegean islands is a magnificent experience. To find a reputable broker, make enquiries at the National Tourist Organization (see p.134). You could also check out the ads which are placed in the English-language press (see p.128), or alternatively try the Hellenic Professional Yachting Association, Akti Themistokleous 22, Piraeus; tel. 452-9571.

Skin Diving: the National Tourist Organization (EOT – see p.000) or Amateur Anglers and Maritime Sports Club at Aktí Moutsópoulos in Piraeus (tel. 411-5731) carry up-to-date information. Snorkelling is not very good along the Attica coast.

Water-Skiing: ask about facilities at your hotel desk or at the National Tourist Organization (see p.134). At times a ski school operates at Astír, but at Vouliagméni it's a speciality! For more information, contact the Water-Skiing Federation, Stournara 32; tel. 523-1875 or 522-9279. The Saronic Gulf islands also offer some good water-skiing.

OTHER SPORTS

Water Polo: for information, contact the Hellenic Athletic Swimming Federation at Jean Maureas (Zan Moreas) 40 in Athens; tel. 922-7922/4.

Tennis: there are tennis courts at all the GNTO public beaches, as well as at many municipal athletic centres, and at the Agios Kosmas athletic centre, where you can rent racquets (tel. 894-8900). Enquire at the tourist office, or alternatively contact the EFOA, Fokionos Negri 9; tel. 865-2908.

Golf: you'll find an 18-hole course at the Glyfáda Golf Club, which is just past the airport (see p.117). A visitor's membership is available for a limited period, and golf carts, clubs and caddies can also be hired. For further information, telephone 894-6820. It's not uncommon for golfers here to wear ear-plugs to lessen the noise of jets nearby.

Horse Riding: there are various riding clubs in the area. Try the Hellenic Riding Club, Paradissou 18, Maroussi, tel. 681-2506 or 682-6128; or the Athens Riding Club, Gerakas, Agia Paraskevi, tel. 661-1088.

Mountaineering: at Bafi (altitude 1,413m or 4,636ft) on Mount Parnes, an alpine refuge hut offers accommodation for up to a hundred people at once. For further information, get in touch with the Hellenic Federation of Mountaineering Clubs, Karageorgi Servias 7; tel. 323-4555.

Snow Skiing: winter sports facilities, including a ski-lift, are located on Mount Parnassus. Further information is available from the Greek Alpine **101**

Club – contact them through your hotel desk in Athens, or go directly to their office in Aráchova. The Hellenic Federation of Skiing Clubs at Agiou Konstantinou 34 (tel. 524-0057) also has information on skiing and mountaineering.

SPECTATOR SPORTS

Football: international soccer and competition in the Greek football league takes place at the huge Karaïskáki stadium near Piraeus. For tickets, see your hotel desk, but be prepared to pay highly for seats, since football is Greece's number-one sport. To reach the stadium, you can take the Metro to the Néo Fáliro stop.

Horse racing: the Athens Race Course (*Ippódromos*) is located at the bottom of Syngroú, just before the sea. Racing with betting is on three times a week – every Monday, Wednesday and Saturday, but hours vary with the season. Restaurants and snack bars are found on the premises.

Entertainment

Athens' after-dark entertainment is vibrant and varied, and carries on long into the night. It usually begins with a meal. For a pleasant and inexpensive evening, head for one of the many tavernas that are located in Plaka. Choose a romantic garden spot or an outdoor table where you can watch the passing scene, and enjoy a leisurely meal to the accompanying strains of Greek music.

Many tavernas – several in Plaka and various others outside the centre – organize live music and/or **floor shows** with traditional folk dancing. Some, however, cater for large tour groups. These are best avoided – the food is mass-produced and you're unlikely to get a good seat. Ask at your hotel desk for a recommendation.

The weekly English publication, *Athenscope* , lists many tavernas as well as bars, piano bars, discotheques and **live music** venues offering a wide range of styles, from rock to blues. If you flick through a copy of the Greek publication

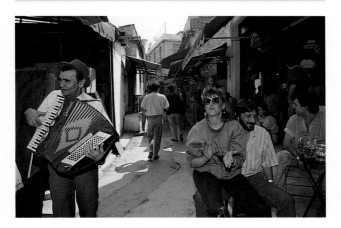

Athinorama, however, you'll be astounded at the breadth of entertainment on offer. You will need a Greek friend to translate – not only the words themselves, but the particular varieties of music which are unique to Greek popular culture. Most visitors never get beyond the ubiquitous strains of *Zorba the Greek* which are heard throughout the tourist areas, but if they sense a genuine interest, most Athenians are pleased to enlighten you on the exciting and beautiful musical traditions of their coun-

Musical entertainment can be found just about anywhere on the streets of Athens.

try, which range from *rembétika* to folk songs to the revolutionary music made popular by Mikis Theodorakis.

The fashionable **nightclubs**, which feature *bouzoúki* music and popular Greek singers are only open in winter in the centre of Athens. After Easter, they transfer to the summer **103**

FESTIVALS AND EVENTS

For up-to-the-minute information on current events, consult the local press (see p.128).

1 January   *Protochroniá* – New Year's Day or St Basil's Day; you may be offered a sprig of basil, a symbol of hospitality.

6 January   *Epiphany* – the priest throws the Pastoral cross into the local harbour and the young men dive to retrieve it.

February   *Carnival* – for three weeks. Masked characters in Athens visit the poor quarters of the city and dance around a maypole.

Clean Monday   *First day of Lent* (movable date). Thousands come together to eat fish soup and beans, and dance on Pnyx hill.

25 March   *National holiday* – celebrated to remember the 1821 revolution against the Turks.

Orthodox Easter   *Páscha* (movable dates) – from Good Friday through to Easter Monday. Candlelight processions, rituals, feasts and festivities.

1 May   *Protomagía* (Festival of spring) – locals hang wreaths on the front doors of their houses to celebrate the new season.

June-September   *The Athens Festival* – drama, opera, music and dance by Greek and foreign artists.

July-September   *Wine festivals* – held at Dafni, around 11km (7 miles) from Athens, with singing, dancing and a large variety of Greek wines.

3 October   *Feast of St Dionysus the Areopagite* – the feast of Athens' patron saint.

28 October   *'Óchi' ('No') Day* – a national holiday.

24, 31 December   *Christmas Eve and New Year's Eve* – celebrated with carol singing in the streets.

clubs along the coast, near the airport and at Glyfáda. These are fairly expensive, with high cover charges and drink minimums, and reservations are required for some clubs. Doors open at 10pm, but the show really gets going around midnight and carries on well into the early morning. Exuberant Greeks, carried away with admiration for favourite singers, are wont to throw plates on the dance floor. Luckily for the nightclub owners, gardenias have now come to be regarded as the ultimate compliment! Far less opulent are the Fáliro *bouzoúki* spots at Tzitzifiés (8km/5 miles from Syntagma along the bay toward Piraeus), which can be recommended for their earthiness.

Most first-time visitors take in the **Sound and Light show** staged outdoors on the hill of the Pnyx. The English version starts at 9pm, the French and German versions at 10pm.

After the 45-minute presentation, you can stroll to the **Dora Stratou Theatre** across the way on the Filopáppou Hill. The Greek dances, musical instruments and costumes are splendidly authentic and the company is internationally known. Nightly performances are held at 10.15pm from the end of May through the summer, with 'matinées' Sunday and Wednesday at 8.15pm.

The Athens **theatre** season is in full swing from November until Easter (most productions are in Greek). The city also has a number of **dance** troupes presenting ballet, folk, jazz, modern and experimental performances. During summer the Athens Festival presents opera, music, ballet and ancient drama at the Odeon of Herodes Atticus (see p.40). Theatre and music concerts by Greek and foreign artists are held at the Lycabettus Theatre on Mount Lycabettus. English productions are presented only occasionally for such festivals.

Cinemas can be found all around greater Athens, and the majority of films are shown in the original English or French versions with Greek subtitles. The open-air summer cinemas, which are set up on roofs, in empty lots and gardens or in

105

actual theatres, are very popular with visitors. There's one in the centre of Plaka. The flourishing Greek cinema industry also produces some good films.

There is a large **casino** on the summit of Mount Parnitha (Parnes), which is 35km (22 miles) from the city centre. You can drive up the winding road or take the cable car from the base, which leaves every half hour. The casino is open

They don't make them like they used to – old-fashioned laternas offer musical delights for all ages.

7pm-3am daily, but closed on Wednesday. You must be well dressed and have your passport with you to get in.

Children

The Greeks love children, and your little ones will be welcomed, smiled at, fawned over, even snatched up and hugged if they'll allow it.

Simple treats are easy to find – a bright balloon, a *laterna* player cranking out hurdy-gurdy tunes, or even a giant sesame-covered pretzel. In the centre of the National Garden is a small zoo with a talking mynah bird, while an aquarium with exotic fish and a crocodile can be found at the Agios Kosmas sports centre, opposite the airport (tel. 894-5640).

The weekly English publication *Athenscope* lists current children's activities. If there's a performance of the shadow puppet theatre (increasingly rare) try and attend. The comic characters are a delightful and traditional form of Greek entertainment for all ages.

Eating Out

Excellent natural ingredients are at the heart of Greek cuisine. Crisp Greek salads, delicious grilled fish, spitted meat and exquisite fruit have good, fresh flavour, and you can always dine in a pleasant, outdoor setting.

Try out the more interesting specialities as well: garlic-yoghurt-cucumber dip (*dzadzíki*), garlic mashed potatoes (*skordaliá*), fried octopus, goat's-milk cheese (*féta*) steeped in olive oil and brine, and the obligatory resin-flavoured wine (*retsína*). If you visit Athens at Christmas or Easter, or are invited to a local wedding, don't flinch at tasting innards soup (*magirítsa*) – in fact, you'll be considered rude if you fail to mop up your plate.

Fine French cuisine, along with seafood, pizza and hamburgers, provide culinary variety. With so many restaurants and *tavérnes*, you won't want to be confined to a full-board plan at a hotel (where the menu is likely to be routinely 'continental'). Several of the very best eating places are located in residential quarters away from the standard tourist haunts – ask an Athenian for the best local addresses.

Don't worry about any possible language difficulties: in most Greek restaurants it is common practice for the customer to be invited into the kitchen to inspect the array of pots and pans simmering on the stove. When you've decided what you'd like, just point it out. A half-portion is *olígo* (a little). Alternatively, you can always ask for a menu (which is usually printed in at least one major European language as well as Greek).

Both restaurants and *tavérnes* open as early as noon, but don't get very crowded before 2pm. Dinner is served from 8pm, but most Greeks eat considerably later. Restaurants in town or in the cooler surrounding countryside are still going long past midnight. Hotels try to maintain earlier mealtimes.

Service charge is included in the bill, but it's customary to leave a tip for the waiter. If a **107** youngster brings iced water or an ashtray, or even just cleans off the table, it's usual practice to give him a few drachmas as you leave.

Should you be lucky enough to be invited to a Greek home for a meal, don't forget to wish your fellow diners 'kalí órexi!' ('bon appétit') before you start to eat.

Finding your way around both the streets and the food are two pastimes which go hand in hand.

Greek Specialities

Greek cooking is simple and at times imaginative, using a few basic ingredients and herbs for flavouring. Olive oil, lemon, tomatoes, onion, garlic, cheese and such herbs as oregano are typical features of the culinary landscap. There may also be Turkish or Arab influences.

Most restaurants of all categories will serve these dishes:

Soúpa avgolémono: this is the Greek's best-known soup: eggs and rice, chicken or meat stock, flavoured with lemon

juice. Delightfully refreshing, it can be served just before the last course (to settle the stomach). A similar sauce is made with eggs and lemon, and usually appears with other dishes.

Dzadzíki: a yoghurt dip with garlic and finely sliced cucumbers. It's served cold, usually with other *mezédes* (appetizers) and bread.

Taramosaláta: this spread is made with *taramá* (grey mullet roe), which is beaten into a pink paste with mashed potatoes, olive oil, lemon juice or sometimes moistened bread. Greeks eat it on bread chunks or on lettuce as a salad.

Dolmádes: these are grape leaves filled with minced meat (often lamb) and/or rice, and seasoned with herbs and grated onion. They're often served hot with an *avgolémono* sauce.

Keftédes: meatballs, usually of minced beef and lamb, with grated onion, oregano, crushed mint leaves and cinnamon, either baked or deep-fried in oil. Regional variations are stewed in tomato sauce and herbs.

Moussaká: one of the most popular Greek dishes. Alternate layers of sliced aubergine (eggplant) and minced meat baked with a white sauce and grated cheese.

Kolokíthia gemistá me rizi ke kimá: this is marrow (zucchini) filled with minced meat and rice.

Finally, *Kotópoulo psitó (sti soúvla)* is spit-roasted chicken.

Seafood

Excellent seafood can be sampled all over Athens, but you'll enjoy it most at Piraeus' little yacht harbour of Mikrolímano (see p.62). A string of dockside restaurants offer seamen's *mezedákia* – octopus chunks, clams, oysters, sea urchins and whitebait – and *psarósoupa* or *kakaviá* – a fisherman's soup that rivals well-known cousins around the Mediterranean. For a local speciality, try *garídes giouvétsi* – shrimps in tomato sauce with *féta*, all cooked in white wine and served in an earthenware pot.

A less known but more reasonably priced seafood row is in Piraeus at Freatis, around from the Zea marina yacht **109**

*S*eafood lovers can take their pick from the day's catch. There's more than enough to go around.

all the frisky, fresh fish, you may see others stored in drawers of the huge refrigerators. They've been frozen to prevent spoiling, a common practice to avoid waste in this hot climate. If the day's catch had to be frozen, no one will try to hide the fact. Fresh – or freshly frozen – fish and seafood are decidedly expensive, since the boats must go ever further to find worthwhile catches.

Among the most common items on Athens menus are: *astakós*, a Mediterranean lobster or crayfish, usually served with oil and lemon sauce or garlic mayonnaise. (Clawless or not, the price is very high.) *Barboúni*: red mullet, considered by Greeks to be the best fish, is normally dusted with flour and fried (it's also expensive). *Chtapódi*, or octopus, is sliced, and then boiled or fried. *Fagrí*, sea bream, is baked. *Garídes* are shrimps; *Glóssa*, sole (smaller than the oceanic variety); *Kalamaráki*, squid, tasty and often tender. *Kéfalos* is grey mullet; *Lithríni*, spotted bream; *Marídes*, whitebait, similar to the Atlantic sprat.

basin, which also has a good cliffside view of the sea.

Fish in Greece is usually grilled or fried, basted with oil and served with lemon juice. You can go into the kitchen, choose your fish and have it weighed in front of you; the **110** price is by the kilo. Aside from

Other Courses

Practically every restaurant in the country serves the reliable Greek 'village' salad (*saláta choriátiki*) of sliced cucumbers, tomatoes, green peppers, onions, radishes and olives, topped with *féta*. If you prefer, you can have a separate order of any of these ingredients. In many *tavérnes*, you dress your own salad with olive oil and a dash of vinegar (Greeks usually dispense with the latter).

Fresh fruit is a real delight. *Pepóni* (a melon tasting somewhere between cantaloupe and honey dew) and *karpoúzi* (watermelon) are mouth-watering, as are the oranges, figs (best in August), peaches and seedless grapes. You can order a bowl of mixed fruit for any number of people – it should come peeled, cut and ready to eat.

The ubiquitous *féta* is the most distinctive Greek cheese, but hard yellow types – *kaséri*, *kefalotíri*, *kefalograviéra* or *kapnistó* – available in many restaurants and shops are good for snacks. Better restaurants may have imported cheeses.

Snacks

In Athens, you'll find an appetite just walking along the street. The delicious smells wafting from snack bars tempt you in, while the sweets, nuts and fruits of the vendors are difficult to resist – pistachio nuts are a local favourite.

At a *psistariá* (specializing in grilled foods), you'll find the usual favourite *souvlákia* – pieces of veal, lamb or pork and vegetables cooked on a skewer (*soúvla*). Even better, and more portable, is *souvláki me pita* – grilled meat, onions, tomatoes and peppers topped with *dzadzíki* and wrapped in round, flat bread (*píta*). *Donér kebáb* or *gyros* (slices off a large cone of meat roasted on a spit), are much tastier than the versions you find at home. You can also get spicy sausages and patties of minced meat in various shapes. You can buy a take-away *souvláki píta* at any time of the day and munch it while strolling through Plaka. If you want to sit at a table, you'll have to order a pricier combination plate.

111

For less piquant treats, go to a *galaktopolío*, a dairy counter selling milk, butter, delicious natural yoghurt and pastries, including cheese-filled *tirópita*. At these shops you can get the makings of a do-it-yourself Greek breakfast: honey to go with your yoghurt, a plastic spoon, and crusty bread. Then repair to a nearby café table and enjoy the morning sun.

Cafés

When in Athens, take time to relax and people-watch. Join the Athenians, who love to sit at cafés, drink a coffee or an aperitif, stare and gossip.

With your drink you'll be served a tiny plate of *mezédes* (hors d'œuvre) – cheese, salami, olives, tomatoes, *taramosaláta* or slices of fried octopus. The *mezé* will vary according to the quality of the café, but it will always appear when *oúzo,* the national drink, is served.

Some cafés and tea-shops serve sweets. For the best sample, look for a *zacharoplastío* (pastry shop). The best known treat is *baklavá*, which is flaky,

paper-thin *fíllo* pastry, filled with chopped walnuts and almonds and drenched in honey or syrup. *Kataífi* may look like shredded-wheat cereal, but the similarity stops there: it, too, is made of *fíllo* and honey.

Ice-cream is popular and excellent in Greece, and is served in various ways in cafés and tea-shops. A *graníta* – scoops of home-made water ice – will be less filling.

Drinks

Clear, aniseed-flavoured *oúzo* – reminiscent of the French *pastis* – has a kick to it. Drink it in moderation and nibble something at the same time, as the Athenians do. It's normally mixed with cold water (turning a milky colour), but can be drunk neat (*skéto*) or, most refreshing, with ice (*me págo*). Whisky, gin and vodka are expensive. The Greeks produce good sweet and dry vermouth.

A good *retsína*, the Greek's classic, tangy white **wine**, can be as smooth and exotic as any other. The Greeks have been drinking it for centuries. Greek wines were originally carried and stored in pine-wood casks, sealed with resin. Later, when vats and bottles replaced the casks, the Greeks continued to resinate their wines to obtain this special flavour.

The Athens region's *retsína*, particularly that from the villages of Koropi and Pikérmi, is renowned as the genuine article, but there's not much of it left. Much of today's *retsína* is chemically aged, and instant resin flavour added from the old-fashioned pine barrels.

Rosé wine, known locally as *kokkinélli*, is considered a delicacy. The one to ask for is *Céllar*, which also produces a non-resinated white wine.

If you decide you'd rather stick with the more traditional wine flavour, there are many very adequate Greek choices. *Sánta Hélena* is a good dry white; Pallíni (a village in Attica) produces tender grapes that rival some French whites. *Boutári* and *Náoussa* – reds and whites – often grace Greek tables. Both *Deméstica* reds and whites are popular and are sold in wine shops abroad.

Greek beer (*bíra*) has German origins and is excellent. Well-known European breweries bottle beer in Greece.

The most common foreign after-dinner drinks are available (but expensive) in Athens.

The breezy roof gardens and lively pavement tables of Plaka's tavernas are perfect for relaxing.

Greek brandies, which tend to be rather sweet, are cheaper.

If you would prefer something non-alcoholic, there are cola drinks and good bottled orange and lemon (*portokaláda, lemonáda*). Greek coffee is boiled to order and comes in a long-handled copper or aluminium pot known as a *bríki* and poured, grounds and all, into your little cup. The thing to ask for is *ellinikó*, served *éna varí glikó* if you want it sweet; *éna métrio*, medium; or *éna skéto*, black. Don't forget to wait a few minutes before sipping to allow the grounds to settle. Traditionally, a glass of cold water is served along with the coffee.

Instant coffee, which is referred to everywhere as *nes*, is also available, while some better cafés also serve espresso. Iced coffee, called *frappé*, is a popular hot-weather refresher. You can also get a cup of tea almost everywhere.

The common toast when drinking is *stin igiá ('ya') sas*! meaning 'cheers!'. A reply to any toast, in the sense of 'the same to you', is *epísis*.

To Help You Order

Could we have a table? **Tha boroúsame na échoume éna trapézi?**

I'd like a/an/some ... **Tha íthela ...**

beer	**mía bíra**	mineral water	**metallikó neró**
bread	**psomí**	napkin	**petseta**
coffee	**éna kafé**	potatoes	**patátes**
cutlery	**macheropírouna**	rice	**rízi**
dessert	**éna glikó**	salad	**mía saláta**
fish	**psári**	soup	**mía soúpa**
fruit	**froúta**	sugar	**záchari**
glass	**éna potíri**	tea	**éna tsäï**
ice-cream	**éna pagotó**	(iced) water	**(pagoméno)**
meat	**kréas**		**neró**
milk	**gála**	wine	**krasí**

114

BLUEPRINT
for a
Perfect Trip

An A–Z Summary of Practical Information

Listed after many entries is an equivalent Greek expression, usually in the singular, plus various phrases that may be useful.

A

ACCOMMODATION (See also CAMPING on p.118, YOUTH HOSTELS on p.139, and the list of RECOMMENDED HOTELS starting on p.66).

Hotels (*xenodochío*). There are six official categories, ranging from L (luxury) at the top, and then A down to E. Rates are set by the government in all categories except 'L', and are posted behind each bedroom door. All rooms in categories L to C have private bathrooms. Grade, however, is not always a good guide to standard, as it may be based on bedroom size, for example, rather than level of comfort. Prices may not include extras such as air-conditioning, high-season surcharge and VAT. Out of season, though, prices may drop by 40%.

Rooms (*domátia*). These range from a bedroom in a family house to a studio flat, and are found especially on islands, where locals tout for business as you disembark. They are graded A to C, and are usually clean and cheap. They may be hard to find around 15 August, when Assumption Day (*tis Panagías*) is celebrated all over the country. Rates and terms for rooms in private homes are often negotiable.

Self-catering. Accommodation ranges from the simple to the luxurious. The better options may be isolated, making car rental essential.

It's a good idea to book your **hotel** room or **villa** in advance. If you arrive without a reservation, contact the Greek Chamber of Hotels at the airport to find a room. A similar office is open until late at night in the National Tourist Organization's central information bureau inside the National Bank of Greece building at Karagiórgi Servías 2, just off Syntagma Square. If you arrive without accommodation after the tourist office has closed, call the tourist police on **171**.

I'd like a single/double room.	**Tha íthela éna monó/dipló domátio.**
with bath/shower	**me bánio/dous**
What's the rate per night?	**Piá íne i timí giá mía níkta?**

AIRPORTS (ΑΕΡΟΔΡΟΜΙΟ – *aerodrómio*)

Athens' airport, **Hellinikon**, 15km (9 miles) from the capital, has two separate terminals reached by different buses; the East Terminal, serving all international and charter flights by international carriers, and the West Terminal, handling only Olympic Airways (the Greek national airline). Domestic flights are operated solely by Olympic.

Both terminals have a bank for currency exchange (West Terminal 7am-11pm, East Terminal 24 hours), hotel-reservation counters, news-stands, car-rental agencies, snack bars and duty-free shops. Luggage trolleys cost 250drs. The National Tourist Organization (EOT) office, at the East Terminal, is open Mon-Fri 9am-7pm in summer (till 6pm in winter), Sat 10am-5 pm.

You can reach both terminals on Express line no. 91 **buses** from Syntagma Square (in front of the Bank of Macedonia-Thrace) or from Stadiou (near Omonia Square at Aiolou). These are blue and yellow double-decker buses which run every 30 minutes 6am-9pm; every 40 minutes 9pm-12.20am; and on the hour 1.30am-5.30am. Express Line 19 connects the airport terminals with Piraeus (Karaiskaki Square); check with the tourist office for times.

The Olympic Airways **bus** for the West Terminal leaves regularly from the Olympic office at 96 Syngrou Avenue. You can also pick it up at Syntagma and Omonia Squares. Check with Olympic for current time schedules. **Taxis** can be hailed at the West Terminal.

Check in at the airport at least one hour before flight departure, and allow plenty of time to get there, especially during rush hour. **117**

ANTIQUITIES (*archéa*)

Certain antiquities may be exported only with the approval of the Greek Ministry of Civilization (tel. 324-3015) and after paying a fee. Anyone caught smuggling out an artifact may receive a long prison sentence and a stiff fine. Travellers purchasing an antiquity should get the dealer to obtain an export permit.

BEACHES (*paralía*)

Because of pollution, it is advisable not to swim any closer to Athens than at Kinétta or Agïï Theódori (55 and 66km, or 34 and 41 miles away) along the northern coast of the Saronic Gulf. On the southern Saronic coast, most Greeks would not swim nearer to Athens than Várkiza. For a cleaner and safer swim, you may prefer the eastern Attica coast, in particular the open beaches around Rafína, Loutsá and Lávrion. Never swim alone, from a beach or a boat.

Most Greeks leave the beach early, lingering in the shade over lunch perhaps, but rarely returning for another swim. As a result, bathing areas are much less crowded in the afternoon, even on Sunday, which is reverentially reserved by Greek families for beach outings. Along all coastal roads, be prepared for heavy Sunday traffic. Boats to Piraeus on Sunday summer evenings are also jammed.

CAMPING (ΚΑΜΠΙΓΚ – *camping*)

Camping is only allowed on organized sites – there are around 20 on the Attica mainland, some open all year. Rates vary depending on season, facilities, and location. For full details contact the EOT office in Syntagma or the Greek National Tourist Office in your country.

May we camp here?	**Boroúme na kataskinósoume edó?**
We've a tent.	**Échoume mía skiní.**

CAR RENTAL (ΕΝΟΙΚΙΑΣΕΙΣ ΑΥΤΟΚΙΝΗΤΩΝ – *enikiásis aftokiníton*) (See also DRIVING IN GREECE on p.122)

Driving in Athens is not recommended, though you may wish to rent a car for excursions. However, car rental is not cheap, and petrol is among the world's most expensive. A 'fly-drive' deal is cheaper; and if you go on a package holiday, your tour operator may be able to arrange a car for you at a better price. If booking direct with a rental company in Athens, choose an international or large local firm.

Deposits may be waived for credit-card holders and members of large tour groups, who may also obtain a small discount. An International Driving Permit or full licence from your country of residence, held for at least one year, is required. Depending on the model and rental company, the minimum age for car rental varies from 21 to 25.

Third-party insurance is often included, and complete coverage is available for a modest charge. Ask if unlimited mileage is included in the rate. All rates are subject to a stamp duty and local taxes.

| I'd like to rent a car (tomorrow). | **Tha íthela na nikiáso éna aftokínito (ávrio).** |
| For one day/a week | **giá mía iméra/mía evdomáda** |

CLIMATE and CLOTHING

Most of the year Athens has a Mediterranean climate, but temperatures can fall a lot in winter, and July-August can be stiflingly hot.

	J	F	M	A	M	J	J	A	S	O	N	D
Air Temp.												
Max °C	12	12	16	19	25	32	44	38	29	23	20	15
Max °F	54	54	60	66	76	90	110	100	85	74	65	58
Min °C	2	7	8	11	16	19	23	23	19	16	11	8
Min °F	35	44	46	52	60	66	72	72	66	60	52	46
Water Temp. (Piraeus)												
°C	14	14	13	15	18	22	25	25	24	22	18	16
°F	57	57	55	59	64	72	77	77	75	72	64	61

Clothing. Mediterranean Athens tends to be informal, but as in every large city, people dress appropriately for the occasion. During business hours, you'll see just as many suits, ties and city dresses as you would in more temperate climes.

From mid-May until the end of September, Athens is decidedly hot. Pack some light clothing and bring a pair of good sunglasses. A light windbreaker or jacket may come in handy if you're travelling to Delphi or other mountain areas, where sudden showers are always possible, and for boat trips, where a scarf is also useful on deck.

Winter can be chilly and wet, so pack a warm coat. In spring and autumn, evenings often turn cool. Light sweaters, cardigans and a raincoat are recommended.

Lightweight shoes are a must, with non-slippery soles.

COMMUNICATIONS

Post Office (ΤΑΧΥΔΡΟΜΕΙΟ – *tachidromío*). The main post office in **Athens**, at Aiolou 100 near Omonia Square, and branch offices at Syntagma Square and Mitropoleos 60, are open Mon-Sat 7.30am-8.30pm. The Syntagma office is also open Sun 7.30am-1.30pm. A mobile branch opens daily at Monastiráki Square. The post office in **Piraeus** is located at Karaiskaki 59.

For postal information, call 324-0010 (for parcels) and 321-9968 (for letters). For bulky packages and those weighing over 1kg, use the Parcel Post Office at Stadiou 4 (inside the arcade; tel. 322-8940).

The post office clerk is obliged to check the contents of any registered letters as well as of parcels addressed to foreign destinations, so don't seal such mail until it has been 'approved'. You can send letters by Express Mail – a kind of special delivery, which carries a surcharge. Call 321-4609 for information about the service.

Stamps (*grammatósimo*) can also be bought at news-stands and souvenir shops (10% surcharge). Letter boxes are painted yellow.

Mail. If you're not sure where you'll be staying, the main post office has a poste restante service. Mail addressed to a branch post office can be collected Mon-Fri during office hours – take your passport. Mail should be addressed: Name, Poste Restante, Athens, Greece.

Telephones, Telegrams and Fax (*tiléfono*; *tilegráfima*). The Greek Telecommunications Organization's (OTE) head office at Patissín 85 provides a 24-hour service. The branch at Stadiou 15 opens Mon-Fri 7am-midnight, Sat-Sun and holidays 8am-midnight. You can call abroad from here; a meter counter will show how much to pay.

If you need assistance when telephoning, dial **169** for recorded instructions in English, French and German. Dial **161** for an international operator, **162** for an English-speaking international operator and for information on rates. Collect calls can be placed by international operators, but there is usually a waiting period of 1-3 hours.

Blue public telephone booths are for local calls only, while orange ones permit long distance direct dialling in Greece and abroad. You can also make local calls at kiosks. Telecards for the cardphone system can be purchased at kiosks or OTE offices.

Telexes can be sent at the above OTE offices, telegrams at all OTE offices. You can also dictate telegrams by phone; dial **155** (inland), **165** (international). Major post offices (see p.120) can send faxes.

express (special delivery)	**exprés**
airmail	**aeroporikós**
registered	**sistiméno**

COMPLAINTS

Your hotel manager, the proprietor of the relevant establishment or your travel-agency representative should be your first recourse if you have a complaint. If you obtain no satisfaction here, the tourist police (see POLICE on p.132) will listen to your comments. Prices at all hotels and public amusement places are set by the government; if you can prove you have been overcharged, the matter will be settled fast.

CRIME (See also POLICE on p.132)

Use common sense and take the same precautions you would in any large city. It's best to leave valuable jewellery and possessions at home, but if you must bring them, lock them in the hotel safe along with your passport and cash rather than leave them in your room. Watch out for pickpockets on crowded public transport.

Possession of drugs is a serious matter in Greece. Make sure you have a prescription from your doctor if you'll be carrying syringes, insulin, any narcotic drugs or codeine, which is illegal in Greece.

CUSTOMS and ENTRY FORMALITIES

EU residents only need an identity card to enter Greece. Citizens of most other countries must have a valid passport. European and North American residents are not subject to any health requirements.

Duty-free allowance. As Greece is part of the European Union, free exchange of non duty-free goods for personal use is permitted between Greece and the UK and the Republic of Ireland. However, duty-free items are still subject to restrictions: check before you go. For residents of non-EU countries, restrictions are as follows: **Australia**: 250 cigarettes or 250g tobacco, 1l alcohol; **Canada**: 200 cigarettes and 50 cigars and 400g tobacco; 1.1l spirits or wine or 8.5l beer; **New Zealand**: 200 cigarettes or 50 cigars or 250g tobacco, 4.5l wine or beer and 1.1l spirits; **South Africa**: 400 cigarettes and 50 cigars and 250g tobacco, 2l wine and 1l spirits; **USA**: 200 cigarettes and 100 cigars and 2kg tobacco, 1l wine or spirits.

Currency restrictions. There are no restrictions for EU residents. Non-EU residents may import up to 100,000drs and export up to 20,000drs (in denominations no larger than 5,000drs). There is no limit on the foreign currency or traveller's cheques you may import or export as a tourist, though amounts in excess of $1,000 or its equivalent should be declared to the customs official upon arrival.

D

DRIVING IN GREECE (See also CAR RENTAL on p.119)

To bring your car into Greece you'll need: a valid driving licence (see below); car registration papers; a nationality plate or sticker; insurance coverage (the Green Card is no longer obligatory, but comprehensive coverage is advisable).

Normally, you're allowed to drive a car in Greece for up to four months on your ordinary licence, provided it has been held for one year. An international driving licence (not required for holders of a British licence) can be obtained through your motoring association.

Driving regulations. Drive on the right and pass on the left. The Greeks have a habit of not always returning to the near-side lane, and of passing on right or left indiscriminately. Traffic from the right has right of way. If a driver flashes his or her lights, it means 'Stay where you are'. A standard red warning triangle is required for emergencies. Seat belts are obligatory, as are crash helmets for motorcyclists.

In Athens. To ease pollution in the city centre, the government has introduced restrictions on driving that apply to local cars, including rented vehicles. Private vehicles with odd-numbered number plates (licence plates) can circulate in the town centre on odd-numbered days of the month (1st, 3rd, and so on), even-numbered plates on even-numbered dates. The restrictions apply on weekdays till 8pm.

Speed limits. Greek motorways (expressways) are good, with tolls levied by distance. Secondary roads are not so good. The main dangers are poor grading, straying livestock, and potholes. Always keep to the right. The **speed limit** is 100kph (60mph) on motorways, 50kph (30mph) in built-up areas and 80kph (50mph) elsewhere.

Parking. As in every other large city, Athens has a parking problem. Parking meters are rife, and infringements severely punished. Some hotels have private garages (which are expensive).

Petrol. Normal-grade petrol (*aplí*, 90-octane), super (*soúper*, 98), lead-free (*amólivdí*) and diesel are all available.

Breakdowns and Accidents. Breakdown assistance is run by the Automobile Association of Greece (ELPA), whose patrols cover the principle routes of the mainland. Their vehicles display the sign: 'OVELPA'/'Assistance Routière ATCC'/'Road Assistance'. Dial **104** for on-the-spot help, and **154** for Express Service road aid.

ELPA's headquarters in Athens is located at Leofóros Mesogíon 2 (tel. 779-1615). They will also provide accident assistance. **123**

Road signs. You may encounter the following written signs:

ΑΔΙΕΞΟΔΟΣ	No through road
ΑΛΤ	Stop
ΑΝΩΜΑΛΙΑ ΟΔΟΣΤΡΩΜΑΤΟΣ	Bad road surface
ΑΠΑΓΟΡΕΥΕΤΑΙ Η ΑΝΑΜΟΝΗ	No waiting
ΑΠΑΓΟΡΕΥΕΤΑΙ Η ΕΙΣΟΔΟΣ	No entry
ΑΠΑΓΟΡΕΥΕΤΑΙ Η ΣΤΑΘΜΕΥΣΙΣ	No parking
ΔΙΑΒΑΣΙΣ ΠΕΖΩΝ	Pedestrian crossing
ΕΛΑΤΤΩΣΑΤΕ ΤΑΧΥΤΗΤΑΝ	Reduce speed
ΕΠΙΚΙΝΔΥΝΗ ΚΑΤΗΦΟΔΙΑ	Dangerous incline
ΕΡΓΑ ΕΠΙ ΤΗΣ ΟΔΟΥ	Roadworks in progress
ΚΙΝΔΥΝΟΣ	Caution
ΜΟΝΟΔΡΟΜΟΣ	One-way traffic
ΠΑΡΑΚΑΜΠΤΗΡΙΟΓ	Diversion (detour)
ΠΟΡΕΙΑ ΥΠΟΧΡΕΩΤΙΚΗ ΔΕΞΙΑ	Keep right

Are we on the right road for ...?	**Ímaste sto sostó drómo giá ...?**
Full tank, please.	**Na to gemísete me venzíni.**
Check the oil/tyres/battery.	**Na elénxete ta ládia/ta lásticha/ti bataría.**
My car has broken down.	**Épatha mía vlávi.**
There's been an accident.	**Égine éna distéichima.**

Fluid measures

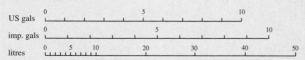

Distance

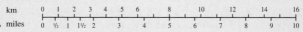

ELECTRIC CURRENT

Athens has 220-volt, 50-cycle AC current. Sockets are either of the two- or three-pin variety.

an adaptor/a battery   **énas metaschimatistís/**
                                       mía bataria

EMBASSIES and CONSULATES *(presvía; proxenío)*

Embassy opening hours vary, so it's best to call first.

Australia: D. Soutsou 37, 115-21 Athens; tel. 644-7303.

Canada: Ioannou Genedíou 1, 115-21 Athens; tel. 723-9511.

Republic of Ireland: Vas. Konstantínou 7, 106-74 Athens; tel. 723-2771.

New Zealand: Semitelou 9, 115-28 Athens; tel. 777-0686.

South Africa: Kifissías 124, 115-26 Athens; tel. 692-2125.

UK: Ploutárchou 1, 106-75 Athens; tel. 723-6211.

USA: Vas. Sofías 91, 115-21 Athens; tel. 721-2951.

EMERGENCIES (See also MEDICAL CARE on p.128 and POLICE on p.132)

In case of loss or theft of your passport or money, contact the police and your consulate (see above). Some key telephone numbers are: Tourist Police: **171**; Police emergency squad: **100**; Ambulance and First Aid: **166**; Emergency doctor: **105**; Fire: **199**.

GAY and LESBIAN TRAVELLERS

Gay bars and events are listed in the weekly publications *Athenscope* (in English) and *Athinorama*.

GUIDES and TOURS (*xenagós; periodía*)

Bilingual, licensed guides to all the museums and sites are available through the guides' association: Somateíon Xenagón, Apollónos 9a; tel. 322-9705. It's a good idea to avoid the 'freelance' guides encountered on site or touting in Syntagma Square.

Tour companies are well-organized and offer many half-day, full-day or longer tours in the city or further afield. Athens' three main companies are Chat Tours (Stadiou 4), G.O. Tours (Voulis 31-33) and Key Tours (Kallirois 4). All offer similar itineraries and can be booked through travel agents or at your hotel desk.

LANGUAGE

It's unlikely you'll have much of a language problem if you stay in accepted tourist areas. Everyone in the tourist industry speaks English, French, German or Italian. Street signs are easy to read: the Greek name is usually accompanied by its Roman equivalent.

To help pronounce Greek street names, we have given their transcriptions. In the case of well-known sites (like Athens and Delphi) and proper names, we've used the time-honoured English spelling.

Stress, an important aspect of Greek, is indicated by an accent (´) above the vowel of the syllable to be emphasized.

Below are listed the Greek letters in their capital and lower-case forms, followed by the letters to which they correspond in English:

A	α	a	as in b**a**r
B	β	v	
Γ	γ	g	as in **g**o*
Δ	δ	d	like **th** in **th**is
E	ε	e	as in g**e**t
Z	ζ	z	
H	η	i	like **ee** in m**ee**t
Θ	θ	th	as in **th**in
I	ι	i	like **ee** in m**ee**t
K	κ	k	

Λ	λ	l	
Μ	μ	m	
Ν	ν	n	
Ξ	ξ	x	like **ks** in thanks
Ο	ο	o	as in got
Π	π	p	
Ρ	ρ	r	
Σ	σ, ς	s	as in kiss
Τ	τ	t	
Υ	υ	i	like **ee** in meet
Φ	φ	f	
Χ	χ	ch	as in Scottish loch
Ψ	ψ	ps	as in tipsy
Ω/ Ω	ω	o	as in got
ΟΥ	ου	oo	as in soup

*except before **i**- and **e**-sounds, when it's pronounced like **y** in yes.

Two words you'll want to learn are ΠΛΑΤΕΙΑ (*platía*), square, and ΟΔΟΣ (*odós*), street, which are often omitted in addresses.

You'll find a list of useful expressions on the inside front cover of this guide. Also helpful is the Berlitz GREEK PHRASE BOOK AND DICTIONARY, which covers many situations you're likely to encounter.

LAUNDRY and DRY-CLEANING
(ΠΛΥΝΤΗΡΙΟ – *plintírio*; ΚΑΘΑΡΙΣΤΗΡΙΟ – *katharistírio*)
Launderettes can be found in the city, some with ironing or pressing facilities. 'Self-service' doesn't always mean just that – you might have to leave your cleaning and come back for it in a day or two.

When will it be ready? **Póte tha íne étimo?**

LOST PROPERTY
If you lose something, you have a chance of getting it back. Enquire at the Tourist Police office, Pireos 154. Should you lose your passport, report it to the police and contact your consulate (see p.125).

I've lost my
wallet/handbag/passport.
**Échasa to portofóli mou/ti
tsánda mou/to diavatirió mou.** **127**

MEDIA

Radio and Television (*rádio*; *tileórasi*). Greek Radio 1 broadcasts a daily weather forecast at 6.30am and the news in English, French, German and Arabic at 7.40am. Reception of the BBC World Service is extremely clear (102.5FM), and Voice of America's English programmes are also easily picked up.

Most hotels have TV lounges. UHF channels carry satellite stations such as CNN (on Channel 16). For Greek folk dancing and music, try Channel 23. French programmes can be seen on TV5.

Newspapers, Magazines, Books (*efimerída*; *periodikó*; *vivlío*). Most European papers – including the British press and the Paris-based *International Herald Tribune* – appear on news-stands in the centre of town, in the afternoon or evening of the day of publication.

There are two English-language newspapers, the *Athens News* (daily except Monday), and *Greek News* (a weekly). The English *Athenscope* (weekly) has comprehensive restaurant, nightclub, cinema and theatre listings, and a directory of useful phone numbers. So does the English *The Athenian* (monthly), though it's hard to find outside the city centre. Details of events are also given in *The Week in Athens* and *This Week in Athens*, available at Syntagma information offices and news-stands (at the latter on sale). The weekly Greek *Athinorama* has the most comprehensive listings of current events.

MEDICAL CARE (See also EMERGENCIES on p.125)

It's always wise to take out health insurance to cover the risk of illness or accident while on holiday. Your travel agent or insurance company at home will be able to advise you.

There's an efficient network of hospitals and clinics in the Athens area. Your hotel receptionist will be able to find a doctor who speaks English – alternatively, ring the consulate. The municipal hospital at Leofóros Mesogíon (tel. 770-1211) runs a 24-hour emergency clinic three days a week. If you telephone on an 'off' day, they will give you the nearest clinic in operation. For an ambulance, call **166**.

Pharmacies (ΦΑΡΜΑΚΕΙΟ – *farmakío*). A red or green cross on a white background identifies a pharmacy (chemist). *Farmakía* open during usual business hours but close on weekends. Each pharmacy displays a notice giving information about night and weekend service, or dial **107**. Your hotel, tour guide, the local English-language press or the tourist police can also assist.

For the import of prescription drugs, see CUSTOMS AND ENTRY FORMALITIES on p.122.

MONEY MATTERS

Currency (*nómisma*). Greece's unit of currency is the drachma (*drachmi*, abbreviated 'drs' – in Greek, ΔΡΑΧΜΕΣ).
Coins: 1, 2, 5, 10, 20, 50, 100 drs.
Banknotes: 50, 100, 500, 1,000, 5,000 drs.

Banks and currency exchange (*trápeza*; *sinállagma*). Banks open Mon-Thurs 8am-2pm, Fri until 1.30pm. Some foreign exchange desks open until 6.30pm. The National Bank of Greece at Syntagma opens Mon-Fri 8am-2pm, 3.30pm-8pm, Sat 9am-2pm. Post offices also have exchange facilities. If changing money, take your passport.

Credit cards (*pistotikí kárta*). Internationally known credit cards are accepted by most hotels, car-rental firms, travel agencies and tourist shops. For dining out, you're better off relying on cash.

Cashpoint machines at major banks accept Visa, Mastercard (Access), Switch (CIRRUS) and some other cards.

Traveller's cheques. All major traveller's cheques are accepted. Always take your passport for identification. Eurocheques are now accepted in many places.

I want to change some pounds/dollars.	**Thélo na alláxo merikés líres/meriká dollária.**
Do you accept traveller's cheques?	**Pérnete 'traveller's cheques'?**
Can I pay with this credit card?	**Boró na pliróso me aftí ti pistotikí kárta?**

129

PLANNING YOUR BUDGET

To give you an idea of what to expect, here are some average prices in Greek drachmas. However, due to inflation all prices must be regarded as approximate.

Airport Transfer. Airport bus to centre 200drs, municipal bus 75drs, taxi 1,500drs (meter starts at 200drs from airport).

Babysitters. 700-1,000drs per hour.

Bus and Metro fares. Bus 75drs, Metro 75-100drs.

Car rental. (international company, high season, July-Sept) *Seat Marbella* 3,800-3,900drs per day, 54-56drs per km. *Opel Kadett* 3,000-4,300drs per day, 37-55drs per km. Add insurance and 18% tax.

Camping. (average prices per day) Adults 660-800drs, children (up to 10) 360-500drs, tents 960drs, cars 400-500drs, caravans (trailers) 1,200-1,400drs.

Cigarettes. Greek brands 320-480drs per packet of 20; foreign brands 450-600drs.

Entertainment. *Bouzoúki* music including a drink 3,000-20,000drs, discotheque (with one drink) 1,500-5,000drs, cinema 1,000-1,500drs.

Hotels (double room with bath, summer season) De luxe 40,000-60,000drs. Class A 12,000-20,000drs. Class B 6,000-14,000drs. Class C 5,000-10,000drs. Class D 3,000-6,000drs.

Meals and drinks. Continental breakfast 1,500drs. Lunch or dinner in a good establishment 6,000-10,000drs; in medium-class 4,000-6,000drs with carafe of wine. Coffee 250-800drs, Greek brandy 300-950drs, beer 300-900drs, soft drinks 200-600drs.

Museums. Adults 400-1,500drs. (See also p.57)

Taxis. Flat rate 1,000drs minimum; metered rate 200drs plus 48drs per km within city limits, double rates in periphery and from midnight to 5am; surcharges are levied for airport, ports, bus terminals, bags, during holiday weeks, and between 5am and 7am.

OPENING HOURS (See also PUBLIC HOLIDAYS on p.132)

Shops. Shops open Mon, Wed, Sat 8.30am-3pm, and Tues, Thur, Fri 8.30am-1.30pm, 5-8pm. Many shops in the tourist areas are open throughout the day and on Sunday.

Museums. Museums open between 8.30 and 10am on weekdays, 10am on Sunday and holidays, and close anywhere from 2 to 7pm depending on the season – later hours being in effect in the summer. Some museums close on Monday, others on Tuesday. Archaeological sites usually have somewhat longer hours. It's best to check the latest schedules on the spot. All museums and sites are closed on major holidays and open only half-days on other holidays (see also MUSEUM HIGHLIGHTS on p.57).

Banks. See MONEY MATTERS on p.129.

Post Offices. See COMMUNICATIONS on p.120

PHOTOGRAPHY and VIDEO

There are photo shops selling major brands of colour and black-and-white film at reasonable prices. Tourist souvenir shops also sell film, but it's best to buy from a photo shop to ensure that the film is fresh and has been properly stored (not exposed to high heat or left sitting in the sun). Photo shops also sell blank tape for video cameras.

Hand-held cameras without flash may be used in most museums and on archaeological sites, although some impose an extra charge. It will cost you an extra 1,000drs at many sites and museums to use your video camera.

I'd like a roll of film for this camera.	**Tha íthela éna film giaftí ti michaní.**
video tape	**miá vídeo-kasséta**

POLICE (astinomía)
(See also CRIME on p.121 and EMERGENCIES on p.125)
Athens has three types of police. The *touristikí astinomía* (tourist police) wear grey uniforms with flags on their jackets identifying the languages they speak. They help visitors and accompany inspectors to hotels and restaurants. If you have a complaint or want information, call **171** (24 hours) or go to Dimitrakopoulou 77; tel. 902-5992.

The rural police, *chorofílakes*, operate outside the city boundaries. They wear green uniforms, shoulder cordons and white helmets.

Athens has its own municipal police force, the *astinomía póleon*; in summer their uniforms are greyish green, in winter green.

PUBLIC HOLIDAYS (argíes)
Banks, offices and shops are closed on the following holidays:

1 January	*Protochroniá*	New Year's Day
6 January	*ton Theofaníon*	Epiphany
25 March	*Ikostí Pémti Martíou (tou Evangelismoú)*	Greek Independence Day
1 May	*Protomagiá*	May Day
15 August	*Dekapendávgoustos (tis Panagías)*	Assumption Day
28 October	*Ikostí Ogdóï Oktovríou*	Òchi ('No') Day, commemorating Greek defiance of Italian ultimatum and invasion of 1940
25 December	*Christoúgenna*	Christmas Day
26 December	*défteri iméra ton Christougénnon*	St Stephen's Day
Movable dates:	*Katharí Deftéra*	1st Day of Lent: Clean Monday
	Megáli Paraskeví	Good Friday
	Deftéra tou Páscha	Easter Monday
	Análipsis	Ascension
	tou Agíou Pnévmatos	Whit Monday ('Holy Spirit')

In addition to these national holidays, Athens celebrates its patron saint's day – *tou Agíou Dionisíou* (St Dionysios the Areopagite) on October 3 – as a legal holiday.

Note: The dates on which the movable holy days are celebrated often differ from those in Catholic and Protestant countries.

R

RELIGION
The national church of Greece is Greek Orthodox. Visitors of certain other faiths will be able to attend services at the following places:

Catholic: St Denis, Venizélou 24; tel. 362-3603. Mass in Latin.

Protestant: St Paul's (Anglican), Filellínon 29; tel. 721-4906. Services in English.

St Andrew's Protestant Church (non-denominational), Papanikole 3, Papagou; tel. 652-1401. Services in English.

Jewish: Beth Shalom Synagogue, Melidóni 8; tel. 325-2823. Services in Hebrew.

T

TIME DIFFERENCES
The chart below shows the time difference between Greece and various cities. In summer, Greek clocks are put forward one hour.

	New York	London	**Athens**	Jo'burg	Sydney	Auckland
winter:	5am	10am	**noon**	noon	9pm	11pm
summer:	5am	10am	**noon**	11am	7pm	9pm

TIPPING
By law, service charges are included in the bill at hotels, restaurants and tavernas. The Greeks aren't tip-crazy, but they do expect you to leave a little more – if the service has been good, of course. Even if **133**

your room and meals are included as part of a package tour, you'll still want to remember the maid and the waiter. The waiter will probably have a *mikró* (an assistant, or busboy), who should get a token of appreciation as well. Some general guidelines:

Hotel porter	50-100drs per bag
Hotel maid	100drs per day
Waiter	5-10% (optional)
Taxi drivers	10% (optional)
Tour guide	200-300drs (optional)
Lavatory attendant	50drs

TOURIST INFORMATION OFFICES
(*grafío pliroforión tourismoú*)

The staff of the Greek National Tourist Organization (Ellinikós Organismós Tourismoú, or **EOT**) can be very helpful both before you leave home and while you're in Greece. They have a wide range of reliable brochures and maps in various languages and can advise on hotel prices and addresses, campsites and itineraries. Their headquarters is at Amerikís 2; tel. 322-3111/9, open Mon-Fri 11am-2pm.

Australia: 51-57 Pitt Street, Sydney, NSW 2000;
tel. (02) 241 1663/4/5.

Canada: 1300 Bay Street, Toronto, Ont M5R 3K8,
tel. (416) 968 2220; 1233 rue de la Montagne, Suite
101, Montreal, Que. H3G 1Z2, tel. (514) 871 1535.

UK: 4 Conduit Street, London W1R 0DJ; tel. 071-734-5997.

USA: 645 5th Avenue, New York, NY 10022,
tel. (212) 421 5777; 611 W. 6th Street, Suite 2198,
Los Angeles, CA 90017, tel. (213) 626-6696/9;
168 N. Michigan Avenue, Suite 600, Chicago,
IL 60601, tel. (312) 782-1084.

The main information office is inside the National Bank of Greece at Karagiórgi Servías 2, off Syntagma; tel. 322-2545, open Mon-Fri 8am-8pm, Sat 8am-2pm. There's also one in the General Bank building on Syntagma; tel. 325-2267, and at the airport; tel. 969-9500.

TRANSPORT

Buses and Trolleys. Bus stops are recognized by the sign ΣΤΑΣΙΣ (*stásis*). There's a fairly good city network of buses and yellow trolleys, but at rush hour vehicles can be very crowded, and in summer, uncomfortably hot. Service throughout the city runs from 5am to 1am, although certain buses and trolleys operate all night (more so at weekends). A bus link between Athens (Syntagma) and Piraeus runs 24 hours a day. Municipal buses to nearby swimming areas (Glyfáda, Vouliagméni) along the Soúnion coast road leave regularly from the Záppion stops on Vas. Ólgas Avenue, opposite the gates of the Temple of the Olympian Zeus. The tourist office has current schedules.

You can buy tickets singly or in blocks of 10 from a kiosk. These must be validated inside the bus. A monthly season ticket allows unlimited travel. Neither is valid on the underground.

Metro. (ΗΛΕΚΤΡΙΚΟΣ – *ilektrikós*) Most of Athens' subway system, operating from 5 to 12.45am, actually runs above ground level. It connects the centre of Athens with Piraeus to the south and Kifissiá, a residential suburb, to the north. New subway lines are being laid to serve all parts of the city. It's a good, fast, economical way to go, providing you avoid rush hour. Keep your validated ticket until the end of your journey – to show it at the exit.

Trains. There are two railway stations in Athens, both located on Theodorou Deligianni. The Greek National Railways (OSE) provides a convenient local service to the Peloponnese from Peloponissos Station (*Stathmós Peloponnísou*). To get there catch bus no. 057 from Panepistimiou Street every 15 minutes. A fast connection to Thessaloníki (Salonica) and northern Greece leaves from the major international station, Lárissa (*Stathmós Larísis*). To get there catch yellow trolley no. 1 from Panepistimiou Street, every 10 minutes.

You can get train tickets and seat reservations from the OSE offices at Karólou 1; tel. 522-4563, 522-2491 or Sína 6; tel. 323-6039, 326-4402. Note that a ticket is valid only for a specific train. Try to arrange rail travel in advance; trains are often very crowded.

When's the next train to...?	**Póte févgi to epómeno tréno giá...?**
single (one-way)	**apló**
return (round-trip)	**me epistrofí**

Taxis (ΤΑΞΙ – *taxi*). Taxis are all metered. Most drivers are honest, but some will try it on. Tricks include setting the meter to the 'double' rate; check the small window beside the fare display – it should read '1' for normal trips, '2' for the double rate. Current charges are listed at the tourist office. (See also MONEY MATTERS on p.129)

From Athens/Piraeus to Ekáli, Pérama, Elefsína, Várkiza and Agía Paraskeví, the normal tariff applies. Taxi drivers often prefer to take two or three different parties at the same time, each paying full fare. If the driver picks you up first, you can insist on having exclusive use of the taxi until you reach your destination.

Although there are taxi stands, it's better to get the hotel porter to hail a taxi for you or do it yourself. If a taxi flashes its headlights, it is for hire. Radio cabs are also available; their surcharges depends on how far away you are – get an estimate when ordering. A tip is not necessary, but you can round up the fare to the nearest 50 drachmas.

Ferries. Boats sail to mainland coastal ports, all the islands, and Italy, Cyprus and Turkey. Sailings are frequent (15 daily to Aegina in summer) and their number increases on weekends and holidays. Hydra is just over three hours from Piraeus, Spétses about four. Schedules and fares are posted daily at the tourist information office.

Boats dock at Aktí Posidónos (Poseidon quay), near Piraeus subway. Some take cars. Ask your hotel or travel agent for details.

Hydrofoils go to Aégina, Hydra, Póros, Spétses, Ermióni, Méthana, Leonídion, Monemvassía, Porto Héli, Kyparisía, Kythera, and Néapolis, more frequently in summer. It costs about 50% more than the boat, but takes less than half the time.

Ferry boat services between the Attica mainland and the island of Salamis leave from Pérama, north of Piraeus.

If you want to take your car, you'll have to pay the stated charge plus an extra loading fee.

TRAVELLERS WITH DISABILITIES

Athens has no special services available for disabled travellers, but some travel agencies are able to help with special arrangements.

TRAVELLING TO ATHENS

BY AIR

International flights. Athens airport is served by scheduled flights from around the world and frequent regional services from Europe.

Charter flights and package tours
From the UK and Ireland. There are literally hundreds of package tours available. Many tour operators offer Athens as part of a two-centre holiday, often with a Greek island(s). A popular alternative is to visit Athens and then go on an island cruise. Self-catering is less popular here, but can be arranged (see ACCOMMODATION on p.116).

From North America. Athens is a popular destination from both the USA and Canada and can be visited in a number of ways. There are straightforward flight/hotel arrangements. Athens is often featured in conjunction with other cities, most popularly with London and Paris or Rome. It is also featured as part of 'Classical Greece' tours (often with a cruise add-on), and on Greece/Egypt/Israel tours.

From Australia and New Zealand. There are package tours to Europe, which include Athens, but undoubtedly the most popular tours are those combining a stay in Athens with either Greek or Mediterranean cruising. You will spend anything up to four days in Athens, some tours placing the accent on the classical aspect of Greece.

BY RAIL

From Paris, the only viable route at present goes via Bologna, Brindisi and Patras (the fare includes the ferry crossing Brindisi-Patras).

Anyone under 26 can purchase an Inter-Rail Card which allows one month of unlimited 2nd-class rail travel on all participating European railways; a more expensive version of the Inter-Rail Card is currently available for those over 26 years, valid for 15 days or 1 month, in 19 countries (check details with British Rail International). Senior citizens can buy a RES (Rail Europ Senior) card which allows a 50% reduction. Anyone living outside Europe or North Africa can purchase a Eurailpass before leaving home. People intending to travel a lot by rail in Greece may like to buy a Greek Tourist Card which offers unlimited 2nd-class travel on the lines of the Greek Railways.

BY ROAD
Due to the conflicts in ex-Yugoslavia, it is no longer recommended to make the entire journey from northern Europe to Greece by road. You can, however, reach Greece with your car by driving through France and Italy and then taking one of the Italy-Greece ferries for the final stage of the trip: in summer, car-ferries operate frequently between certain Italian ports and Greece. The most popular routes are Ancona-Patras, Brindisi-Patras and Venice-Piraeus. Advance booking is recommended in high season. A service is also available from Toulon in France to Patras.

Some coach operators offer excursions from London and continental Europe to Athens.

BY SEA
Cargo/passenger services are available from the USA to Piraeus. Departures are approximately three to four times per month, with dates and ports of call subject to cargo requirements. Bookings should be made well in advance.

There are also cargo/passenger services from Southampton to Piraeus. The duration of the voyage is approximately 10 days.

Via Italy, there are crossings from Venice, Brindisi and Ancona.

WATER (neró)
Athens' tap water is perfectly safe to drink. Bottled mineral water, usually still rather than fizzy, is always available.

a bottle of mineral water	**éna boukáli metallikó neró**
fizzy (carbonated)	**me anthrakikó**
138 still	**choris anthrakikó**

WEIGHTS and MEASURES (See also DRIVING on p.124)

Greece uses the metric system.

Length

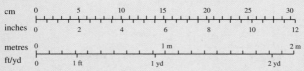

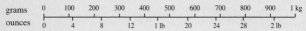

Weight

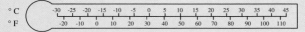

Temperature

WOMEN TRAVELLERS

Single women travellers *will* be pestered by men. As this begins with some friendly chatting, it is hard to avoid without being rude. The best thing is to say you are married. Be ready for unwanted advances.

YOUTH HOSTELS (ΞΕΝΩΝ ΝΕΟΤΗΤΟΣ – *xenón neótitos*)

Members of the International Youth Hostels Association can stay at any of Athens' three hostels or the one in Piraeus. Otherwise, get an International Guest Card at the Greek Association of Youth Hostels, Dragatsaníou 4 (7th floor), off Platía Klafthmónos; tel. 323-4107.

Information and addresses are available from the EOT office at Syntagma. The YWCA (XEN) at Amerikís 11; tel. 362-6180 also offers inexpensive accommodation.

Delphi has a pleasant hostel at: Apollonos 29; tel. (0265) 82268.

Index

Where an entry is referred to more than once, the main one is in **bold**.
Entries in *italics* refer to illustrations.

141

143

Berlitz – pack the world in your pocket!

Africa
Algeria
Kenya
Morocco
South Africa
Tunisia

Asia, Middle East
China
Egypt
Hong Kong
India
Indonesia
Japan
Jerusalem
Malaysia
Singapore
Sri Lanka
Taiwan
Thailand

Australasia
Australia
New Zealand
Sydney

Austria, Switzerland
Austrian Tyrol
Switzerland
Vienna

Belgium, The Netherlands
Amsterdam
Brussels

British Isles
Channel Islands
Dublin
Ireland
London
Scotland

Caribbean, Latin America
Bahamas
Bermuda
Cancún and Cozumel
Caribbean
French West Indies
Jamaica
Mexico
Mexico City/Acapulco
Puerto Rico
Rio de Janeiro
Southern Caribbean
Virgin Islands

Central and Eastern Europe
Budapest
Hungary
Moscow and St Petersburg
Prague

France
Brittany
Châteaux of the Loire
Côte d'Azur
Dordogne
Euro Disney Resort
France
Normandy
Paris
Provence

Germany
Berlin
Munich
Rhine Valley

Greece, Cyprus and Turkey
Athens
Corfu
Crete
Cyprus
Greek Islands
Istanbul
Rhodes
Turkey

Italy and Malta
Florence
Italy
Malta
Milan and the Lakes
Naples
Rome
Sicily
Venice

North America
Alaska Cruise Guide
Boston
California
Canada
Disneyland and the Theme Parks of Southern California
Florida
Greater Miami
Hawaii
Los Angeles
Montreal
New Orleans
New York
San Francisco
Toronto
USA
Walt Disney World and Orlando
Washington

Portugal
Algarve
Lisbon
Madeira

Scandinavia
Copenhagen
Helsinki
Oslo and Bergen
Stockholm
Sweden

Spain
Barcelona
Canary Islands
Costa Blanca
Costa Brava
Costa del Sol
Costa Dorada and Barcelona
Costa Dorada and Tarragona
Ibiza and Formentera
Madrid
Mallorca and Menorca
Seville

IN PREPARATION
Bali and Lombok
Edinburgh
Israel

144

019/502 RV

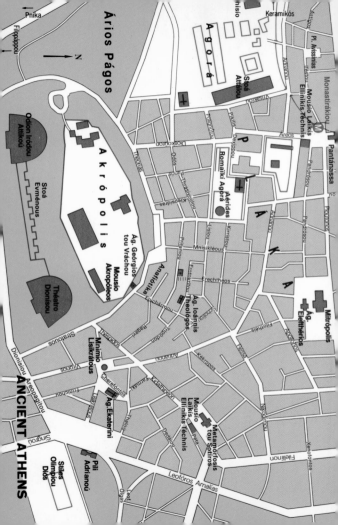

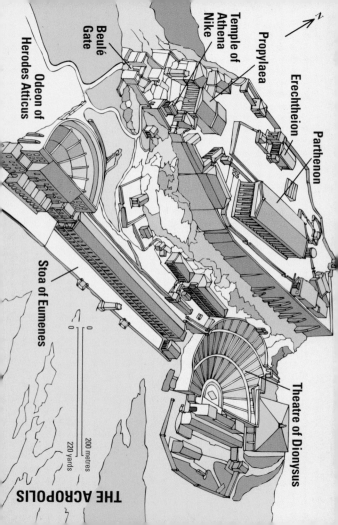

THE ACROPOLIS

Beulé Gate

Temple of Athena Nike

Propylaea

Erechtheion

Parthenon

Odeon of Herodes Atticus

Stoa of Eumenes

Theatre of Dionysus

N

0
0

200 metres
220 yards

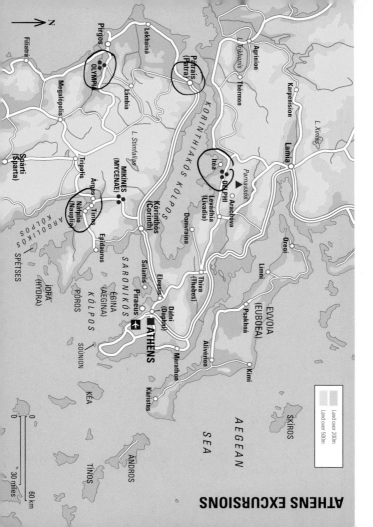

ATHENS EXCURSIONS

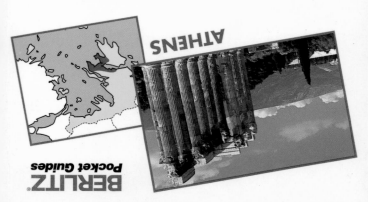

With more than 32 million copies sold, Berlitz Pocket Guides provide a wealth of information in a size that fits every pocket. Each title is carefully researched, fun to read, and easy to use.

Whether you're planning a short trip or an extended visit to Athens, this guide will make your stay more enjoyable, interesting and comfortable.

■ Features colour maps and photographs throughout

■ Details of the best local hotels and restaurants

■ Practical information covering amenities, transportation, emergency help and useful expressions

■ Comprehensive recommendations for shopping, sports, entertainment and nightlife

ISBN 2-8315-1406-1

USA $7.95
Can $8.95
UK £4.95

Ἀγγλικὴ "Ἐκδοση

9 782831 514062